Real Christianity

Real Christianity

Bailey E. Smith

BROADMAN PRESS
Nashville, Tennessee

Dewey Decimal Classification: 248.4
Subject heading: CHRISTIAN LIFE//CHRISTIANITY
Library of Congress Catalog Card Number: 79–50335
Printed in the United States of America.

To the people who have helped me so much to see real Christian living in practice. These are the people who have called me pastor. I love them, each and every one, and thank God for what they have meant to my life.

In Arkansas:

Rehobeth Baptist Church
Brickeys Baptist Church
Jennie Baptist Church
Memorial Baptist Church, Waldo
First Baptist Church, Warren

In Texas:

First Baptist Church, Crowley

In New Mexico:

First Baptist Church, Hobbs

In Oklahoma:

First Southern Baptist Church, Del City

Preface

Real Christianity is a book that I trust will challenge Christians everywhere to total commitment to the Lord Jesus Christ. Each chapter endeavors to set high the standard of Christian excellence. In this day of cut-rate dedication and bargain-basement loyalty, I hope *Real Christianity* will be an oasis in the desert.

Every chapter has as its background the book of Acts—and appropriately so for such a volume. When one examines the single-minded dedication of the first-century church, he discovers a Christian fellowship of believers that has much to teach the stained-glass, air-conditioned, cushioned-pew Christian of this generation. The early church understood what was real about Christianity and gave their every moment to its propagation. Their faith was not a thread that ran through the garment of their life; it was the pattern from which their entire life was built. They believed the words of a song they never heard, one we often hear, but may not really believe.

> Jesus, Jesus,
> Jesus in the morning—
> Jesus at the noontime—
> Jesus, Jesus,
> Jesus 'til the sun goes down.

May I suggest that it would be good for each reader to read the Scripture discussed along with each chapter of *Real Christianity*. For the sake of space often I do not list a Scripture as I refer to a portion of the Scripture being studied in each chapter. For clarity and continuity, it would be helpful to let the Bible be the companion volume for this work.

Let's all pray that Christians everywhere will have a burning desire to be totally at the disposal of the Master. If that day comes, then we all shall see a glorious revival brought about by God's people deciding to live a vital, virile, relevant *REAL CHRISTIANITY.*

Bailey E. Smith, Pastor
First Southern Baptist Church
Del City, Oklahoma

Contents

Real Christianity

1
A Life That Matters

(Acts 9:23-31)

Mrs. Andrev, Russian author of the book *Little Men in Great Days,* said, "We see before us little men in great days. We always felt assured that if any trouble came we could be at ease. Our great men would handle the situation. But what became of our great men? They are little pygmies in this world crisis."

It is no secret today that our world is in need of men and women of greatness—people who live a life of some consequence—a life that matters in the main-stream of life's good. It is a day for maturity and excellence.

> Solomon Grundy
> Born on Monday
> Christened on Tuesday
> Married on Wednesday
> Taken ill on Thursday
> Worse on Friday
> Died on Saturday
> Buried on Sunday
> And that was the end of
> Solomon Grundy

This might well be the biography of some people today, the only difference being, that a few meaningless years have been thrown in between those events. Yet, for us Christians there must be something infinitely more. Life must not be a play-

11

thing where our days and years are only spent marking time. We must come back not only to sing but also to live the words:

> Onward, Christian soldiers,
> Marching as to war,
> With the cross of Jesus
> Going on before!
> Christ the royal Master,
> Leads against the foe;
> Forward into battle
> See his banner go!
>
> —Sabine Baring-Gould

Our day of Communist aggression, moral decay, and godless disrespect for right must be met by lives that matter. Our churches have enough floaters. We need people who are strong enough to fight the contemporary currents.

These words bring us to the book of Acts 9:23-24 where we see a life that mattered—a life no one counted as irrelevant or insignificant. A life that was loved by many and hated by scores. A life you and I would do well to observe.

A Life That Matters Will Stand for Something

When you look at this passage of Scripture, you discover a man who believed with all of his heart that he had something for which to stand. In fact, in verses 29 and 30, you find some very significant phrases. In verse 29 you find "and he spake boldly" and in verse 30 you find, "which when the brethren knew." When those people saw Paul after his conversion—a man who had been tall with anger; a man who had been tall with hatred; a man (though short in stature) who suddenly changed to a man tall in righteousness, tall in goodness, and tall in every kind of Christian endeavor—they finally decided that he was standing for Christ.

Now this is strange, is it not? For there had been many other representatives of Christ and no one ever said "they knew." This man was real. They had seen others come and go and they had seen men come along and say this is the Christ and they would begin to worship Jesus and follow him. But when the test of true discipleship really came, the others fell by the wayside.

This could have happened to Paul. The people could have started saying, "Not only were we afraid of him as Saul but also we don't believe in him much now." The Scripture says that even though they were afraid of him at first, there came a time when Paul preached so boldly and with such confidence, determination, and belief that the "brethren knew" he was for real. They knew without a shadow of a doubt. They knew with every bit of honest belief they had—here a man was standing for something—real Christianity.

Paul spoke boldly and he spoke often. He spoke at every opportunity, and the people knew he was among the disciples of the Lord Jesus. A life that matters stands for something.

Paul was indeed a man who stood for something. He spoke boldly. The apostle Paul spoke boldly not just with his preaching, but his entire life was a bold testimony and these people knew it. Many people, members of churches, have never spoken boldly one time in their lives. They get by on claims of their Christianity and their church membership. They may even serve on a board or committee in their churches. But do their lives really show this kind of transforming, world-changing, kind of bold Christianity? No, not at all.

Paul didn't say, "I may be right." "It is my hypothesis." "It is my consensus." He spoke boldly because Christ was the most important thing in his life. He spoke and stood boldly for the cause of his Lord.

Conviction—we don't hear that word anymore. I used to love to hear preachers and godly deacons talk about people being "under conviction." Now we talk about them "wanting to join the church." Conviction meant that deep down in the heart of somebody he was feeling that some of things

that he was doing; some of the places he was going; some of
the thoughts that he was having were wrong. He knew that
he had to come to the Lord and do something about it. This
is still a need in our day for people to get under the convicting
power of a Holy God.

When the issue of liquor comes up, what's supposed to be
our answer? "Yes, wrong." When it comes to gambling, "Yes,
wrong." When it comes to half-day worship on the Lord's
Day? "Yes, wrong!" Yes, a thousand times so. Cheating, is it
wrong? "Yes." When it comes to immorality, is it wrong?
"Yes." Let's not vacillate or cow down. Let's be bold for
Christ who lived a life of boldness.

Billy Graham recently spoke at a school in California. He
made the statement that what we need, and I quote verbatim,
"is a good, old-fashioned religion of honesty, purity, and decency," and those so-called intellectuals booed him till he
could no longer speak.

We are all going to have to be like Paul and speak boldly
the convictions of morality and truth. We are going to have
to believe with all our hearts that Jesus Christ is more important than the applause of mankind. He, above all else, must
be the most important thing in our lives.

Does your life matter? Does your life matter to your church?
How much would it hurt the church's financial program if
you should suddenly have a heart attack and die? How many
lost people would die and go to hell if suddenly you were
taken from this world? How little would the Sunday evening
crowd be if suddenly you had a car accident and had to leave
this world? Does your life matter? Does it make any difference
in the kingdom of God about you? Are you riding in the boat
while somebody else does the paddling?

Paul spoke boldly because he had a message and a heart
that was burdened with the needs of Christ around the world.
Paul said, "I shall go forward." Christ lived fully and completely and wholly in his life. He mattered. I quoted "Onward

Christian Soldiers" earlier. One of the lines almost makes me weep—"Hell's foundations shall quiver." But I wonder how much, today, you and I are shaking the foundations of hell. Do our lives matter?

A Life That Matters Will Have Its Dangers

Not only does a life that matters stand for something but also a life that matters will almost always be in danger. There is always a price to pay for excellence.

Verse 23 of the Scripture says "the Jews took council to kill him." You find in verse 24, "and they watched the gates day and night to kill him." Now look ahead to verse 29, "and disputed against the Grecians: but they went about to slay him." In just a matter of a few short verses, three references are made to the fact that people wanted to kill Paul. Why? Because he mattered.

You never hear of a football team rejoicing or throwing a party when the player who sits on the bench for the other team gets injured. But they enjoy the fact that the opposing quarterback breaks his arm or has some kind of temporary disease that puts him in the hospital until the game is over. Why? Because it's the man on the field getting hot, sweaty, and dirty who matters.

You know why some of us aren't talked about any more? Because we don't matter. We're not doing the world any harm. We're sitting on the bench for Christ and letting somebody else play the game and get the bumps and get the tackles and get the scars. A life that matters is going to be out where the danger is and that's why some people wanted to kill Paul.

In the Bible you find disciples galore who never once had their lives in danger. You find people who worked for Christ all of their lives and not one time did any one want to kill them. Even some among the original twelve disciples never were in danger of their lives. But a life that matters has its dangers.

We may not have the same danger as the early martyrs, but do you know what the greatest danger in our world is? It's not that the blood will flow from our body but that the testimony will not flow from our Christian influence.

If you are living a life that matters, you're going to have testings. Somebody will say, "Just hold the cocktail glass at least." "Just be part of us." "You're here where nobody can see you." "After all, you're not at church; that comes on Sunday."

The greatest danger I face as a preacher is that I might care more about the applause of the world than I do about the approval of God. And if we are not careful, our testimonies (if we live lives that matter), are going to be in danger. When somebody sees a person on fire for Christ, really living a Christian life, he is going to try to say to that person, "Come down to my level. Get off your mountaintop where the sun shines and get down in the mud with me." But the problem in diving into the mud is that when you stand up and go to the mountaintop, you can't see the sunshine anymore for the mud that covers your eyes. A life that matters is going to be in danger.

Even today men who stand for something often are in physical danger. A pastor friend told me about a preacher of the largest Baptist church in Alaska who was so much after a particular industry, they had put a price tag on his head. If anyone could kill that particular Baptist preacher, they would give the murderer a check for thousands of dollars. There was a reward for the preacher's murder and he had been, indeed, shot at. My friend told of one man who, in an attempt to shoot the preacher, fell out of a window and killed himself.

I challenge you to live for Christ with all of your heart. Live it worthily and be careful. The world has its sinister sarcasm, "You were in Sunday School, I never thought you would do it." "You were in church, well, isn't that sweet." Some people want you to be less than what you ought to be. Live a life that matters. Here are some reasons for living such a life.

A Life That Matters Will Have
the Support of Some Good Men

When Paul was really in trouble; when he was really sweating and about to have the sword across his neck, somebody came to his rescue. Little disciples, probably too cowardly to do any speaking like Paul, probably too cowardly to really step out and stand for something, came with their basket and with their rope. They put Paul in the basket, threw him over the wall, and let him down to safety. But when he went to some of the other disciples, they said no to him. "We don't want anything to do with you," they said. They still thought he was the same Saul of Tarsus, that wicked man who killed Christians.

Notice the interesting statement in verse 27, "But Barnabas took him." That's always true in a Christian life. Let some of the world curse you; let some of the people you thought were your friends spit on your Christian influence, but aid will come—from a true friend. There will always be a Barnabas in your life if you live for Jesus. Always! Even if all the world seems against you, God will send a needed friend.

Paul faced the world, it seemed, alone, but good men came to his rescue, upheld him, and he was able to continue the fight. A life that matters, a life that is significant, a life that counts will always have the support of some good men.

Jesus Christ never did win the applause of all men. In fact, he only won a small group, but I promise you until the day I die, those people whom Jesus won to his cause and to his heart and to his life were the good men of that day—the best men of the first century.

Think of the story of David and Goliath with the cowardly Israelites standing back and Goliath leading the mighty Philistines. David, a little shepherd boy, left his sheep behind, picked up five stones and a slingshot and buried a stone into the forehead of Goliath. He fell and David jumped on his chest, and cut his head from his body. When it was all over some of the Israelites came running to David and said, "David, let us help you, the head is too heavy for a boy. Let us come help you."

Our world is looking for a David who steps out from the multitudes of mediocrity and from the crowds of poor testimony and says, "I will fight the giant." The world is looking for a leader; the world is looking for somebody. The world is not against Christianity, it is just looking for some Christians, people who will step out from the crowd and say, "Show me the giant—I don't care if I live or die. Just put me in the battle." We need people who go forward with faith and say, "Lord, I'm going to do it for thy cause."

When the early Christians were captured and were taken to their places of execution, they would sing Psalm 8:1, "O Lord, our Lord, how excellent is thy name in all the earth." That was their Bible. That was their Scripture. People would peer through the windows of their houses and see Christians going in chains to their deaths. Their testimonies were so great singing the song, "O Lord, our Lord, how excellent is thy name in all the earth," that people would flow from their houses and march with the Christians singing the same song and all of them, the old and the new, would go to their death together.

The reason we don't have more people following Christianity is because we don't have enough Christians who are willing to matter. It's going to take some leadership and some stepping out in faith to matter for Christ. A host of good men will come and join you and say, "Thank God for a man that I could follow—who is following Jesus." That is real Christianity.

2
Love Without Limits

(Acts 9:43; 10)

We don't just need more love in our world; we need the right kind of love. The Bible itself points out that all love is not good. It speaks of a love that kills—the love of the world. The Bible also describes the evil of self-love and love for wrongdoing.

Goethe reminded us that "we are shaped and fashioned by what we love." And Longfellow was hinting at this when he eloquently cautioned, "There is nothing in this life of ours than the first consciousness of love—the first fluttering of its silken wings—the first rising sound and breath of that wind which is so soon to sweep through the soul, to purify or to destroy."

So love, personality's most sought-after virtue, must be channeled in the proper direction. If love is surrounded with clauses and conditions, it is probably not love at all.

The kind of love we Christians must give our world is that selfless, pure, Godlike love. A love that may not always be easy but a love that is always tender and right is the kind of love we must communicate to our world. To accomplish in our world what we are commissioned to do, we must possess a love without limits.

In the book of Acts, chapter 10, there are some appropriate lessons on a limitless kind of love. The word *love* itself, taken in its purest form, implies limitless and abiding affection. Do you and I have limitless and abiding affection without limits?

Probably not. However, we have no other choice than to try to have a love without limits.

Love Without the Limits of Convenience

Acts 9:43, explains, "And it came to pass, that he tarried many days in Joppa with one Simon a tanner." The tanner had one of the most undesirable businesses in the New Testament. A tanner was a person who had to live a great distance from the city because of the nature of his business. His house and his person literally smelled with the results of his work. A tanner pealed the skins from dead animals and prepared the skin to be used by the public for various purposes.

Therefore, when a man like Simon Peter, a Jew, came to realize that Simon the tanner was lost, a man who didn't have Jesus Christ as Savior, Peter had to decide between one of two things. First of all, he could have said to himself, "I can choose to be ostracized from this community and from my friends. I can take on his odor; I can take on his reputation; I can take on association with his kind, if it means someone knowing my Lord." Or, he could have chosen to stay with the acceptable group and forget about the smelly tanner. Peter chose the former.

It was a difficult conclusion for Peter to come to. All of his life Peter, the big, husky man, always had his way with the people who were important. A fisherman he was, and a man who used his hands, but Peter was never given to fooling around with small stuff. The impulsive Simon Peter was a man who wanted to be known and have his name in the lights. He was a man who, when a question was asked to a group, would always scream out the answer. He didn't want to be just one in the number. He wanted to be Mr. Big.

Someone told Simon Peter, "Simon, there is a man who is lost, he doesn't know Christ—but wait a moment Simon, he is a tanner. He stinks—he has been thrown out of his community, you don't want to go see him." Simon had the choice—

so-called decency or heartfelt conviction. Peter chose to be honest to what he knew was right, and he moved in with this man.

Love is not love at all if it is not love without necessary convenience. It was very inconvenient for Simon Peter to give of himself to living in the home of a man who was a tanner and who was an outcast of the community, a man whom nobody really loved because his profession was not as a doctor or an attorney. He was literally a stinking tanner.

There are some people in our world today, some of them sitting in the pews, some of them standing in the pulpit who love people a great deal—until that loving causes them some inconvenience. If it interferes with their plans, forget love. If they can do it professionally, if they can do it without getting their hands dirty, if they can do it without someone looking at them and saying, "Look who he loves," they might show a little concern. But if it takes getting down in the dirt, if it takes really showing heartfelt concern until they become identified as a friend of a lost man that is not socially elite, they will turn their backs.

I can imagine that for awhile Peter had some people talking about him. "What an awful thing for Peter to do—a man who was so proper when speaking at our gatherings. I would have never thought it of him."

It's a temptation for a teacher to visit the people in her class who always come, who are always there, and therefore, she can report on the Sunday School report that she has visited some people. But the difficult ones—she often finds it convenient to leave alone.

A preacher may be tempted to associate with those who are already polished, upright, rich, and stable and can contribute to his own financial being. But the person who loves beyond the limits of convenience is the one who loves people because everyone is a creation of God. It should not matter whether a person has a two-hundred dollar suit on or whether

his toes are sticking from his shoes and he hasn't got a dime
in his pocket.

I've been reading the very beautiful biography of J. Howard
Williams, a great Baptist preacher from Texas, who served
some of the greatest churches of that state and was president
of Southwestern Baptist Theological Seminary in Fort Worth.
On one occasion, Dr. Williams came out of his church and a
man in a long Cadillac came up to him and said, "Preacher,
come on, I want to take you out for a big steak." Almost
simultaneously, a poor little lady and her husband—ragged
as they were, drove up in their jalopy of a car and said,
"Preacher, we don't have much, but come and eat with us."
He said a quick thank you to his rich church member and
quickly climbed into the backseat of the old car. Love without
convenience was evident.

A young mother was sitting in the waiting room of an adoption agency, a little clubfooted girl in her arms. A mother
with a beautiful adopted child began to stare across the room
at the handicapped child. The mother with the little handicapped child noticed the sympathetic looks and stares of pity
they were receiving, so finally the mother who had the little
clubfooted girl in her arms looked over and said, "Don't feel
sorry for us."

The other lady was shocked and said, "Well, I really wasn't,
I just thought what a tragic thing it was that the little girl
had to endure that!"

The mother replied, "No, don't think about that. Do you
know what we are back here for?"

"I guess it's because you want to give this one up and get
one that is whole," the observer stated.

And the mother said, "No, no, no, a thousand times no.
We are here to ask the director of the adoption agency if
he can find us another little clubfooted child. Because children
who are whole, who have all of their fingers and all of their
toes and a healthy body, have people waiting in line to get

them. We have come back to ask God and ask this director to bless us with another handicapped child."

There are people all over our world, in our nation, in our churches who are handicapped financially and socially and with sin in their lives, but if our preachers and our deacons and our teachers and our people don't love them—who will? God help us to love them for what they are no matter the cost.

Love Without the Limits of Self-Appeasement

Simon climbed to the housetop and I think that he must have looked out over the blue Mediterranean waters where the ships were sailing. The sails must have in some way placed themselves into his vision and he saw a great sheet coming down from heaven with all kinds of animals in it. God spoke to him and said, "Rise, Peter; kill, and eat" (10:13). Simon, being a Jew, knew that Jews could not eat particular things. And he said, "Not so, Lord; for I have never eaten any thing that is common or unclean." And God said to him, "What [I have] cleansed, that call not thou common" (10:14-15).

There is a great lesson from this. How often you and I don't love unless the people appeal to us.

William Booth, the great founder of the Salvation Army, encountered a man in the gutter and began to love him and show kindness and concern, but the man began to reject Booth and lie to him. Booth continued to express love and compassion. Everything William Booth did was for love and kindness, and finally the man came and found himself in Christ. When he gave his testimony someone asked him, "How was it that you came from the dirty gutters of our street to be a Christian with a testimony like that?"

The man looked at William Booth and he pointed his finger at him and said, "Kindness and love, kindness and love, kindness and love."

What cruelty cannot do, what law enforcement cannot do,

what the gavel of the judge fails to do, love will always accomplish. "Kindness and love, kindness and love."

The Bible says that if we don't love our brother we cannot love God. When the rich young ruler came to Jesus and said, "What shall I do to inherit eternal life?" (Luke 18:18) Jesus said, "Sell all that thou hast, and distribute unto the poor" (Luke 18:22). But the rich young ruler didn't have enough love for man to have enough love for God in order to be saved. And the Scriptures say that he went away sad. Love must not be based upon self-appeasement.

I saw some young people some time ago laughing at a cripple walking down the main street of our city. I suppose that if he were not crippled, it would have been a funny spectacle, for the movement and the gyrations of his body were certainly not coordinated. You know what I wanted to ask those young people? I wanted to say to them, "Now wait a moment, what did you have to do with being born whole?"

A few years ago in a Baptist church, a visiting preacher preached on Sunday morning. After everybody left he shook hands with a black janitor. The deacons met that afternoon and thought that they shouldn't let the guest preacher preach that night because he had shaken hands with a black man. They finally decided that they would let him preach that night, but they would not ever let him come back to their church again. He's never had another invitation.

When white men talk against men who are red or yellow or black, I want to say to them, who are not like Christ at all, "What did you have to do with being born white?" Not a thing! And yet, often you and I are guilty of calling some people common or unclean while we put our fingers under our vests and brag about what great creations of God we are. If there is any person we would not let have the privilege of God's heaven, we automatically place a question mark over our profession of faith. Love must be without self-appeasement.

I shall never forget attending a service at the First Baptist Church of Waipahu about thirty miles from Honolulu when I was in Hawaii doing summer mission work. I remember hearing a Caucasian preach. I saw a Negro man and a Filipino man taking up the offering. When I walked out, a Chinese man and a Japanese man were greeting people and shaking hands. I thought to myself, What a picture of the universality of the gospel to all men.

In our Scripture passage all of those beasts came down together in the same sheet from heaven. It was a lesson to Peter (and to us all) that all of God's people are not the same color or race, but they all are from God. They are of God's likeness— Jew or Gentile, Greek or barbarian. They are all one for whom Christ died. This was the beginning of a witness to the Gentiles and the vision was sent to convince the Jews to share the good news with Cornelius (a Gentile) and all others.

It is interesting to note Peter's reaction, "Lord, . . . I have never eaten" (author's italics). Peter's problem was much like ours—he said I too often. I must not love people because I find it easy. I must get out of the way and let the love of Christ embrace all people through me, "for ye are bought with a price" (1 Cor. 6:20). A Christian does not love for convenience or self-appeasement. He loves because God is love and he should be Christlike.

Love Without the Limits of Poor Vision

Christ was trying to open the door to the Gentile people and I think he got through to Peter because in this Scripture we find: "And as Peter was coming in, Cornelius met him, and fell down at his feet, and worshipped him. But Peter took him up, saying, Stand up; I myself also am a man" (Acts 10:25-26). Jesus got the lesson over to Peter quite well. But you see, if our vision is poor and if we don't see that some of the minority groups are turning to other religions and lesser interests, we are going to lose any possibility of communica-

tion. While you and I shut our doors and our hearts, not seeing
what all men can be through Christ, something else is winning
other people. We must have a vision of what even the worst
man can be through Jesus.

I wonder what would have happened if somebody had
shown more love to Judas. I wonder what would have happened if some of those disciples who saw his tendency toward
greed would have placed their arms around Judas and said,
"Judas, we know you have a fault, but we love you." Judas
might have written a Gospel. Judas might have become one
of the greatest saints of the Bible. I wonder what would have
happened. But often our vision is too limited to see what
love can really do. We need visions that can see beyond black
skins, sins, and all else in order to see the heart through the
eyes of love.

In Scotland a giant eagle swept into a baby carriage, picked
up a small baby, and flew off with it. The villagers were so
upset they didn't know what to do. Finally on a high and
lofty crag, they saw the eagle perched, and they knew the
baby was there. Someone wired a seaman. He came and tried
to climb the mountain, but as he got a little way up, he looked
down at the jagged rocks beneath him and said, "I cannot
do it," and he came down. They got a professional climber—
a man accustomed to the high slopes and he went up with
his rope and with his pick and with all of the help that he
could, but soon he, also, gave up.

But finally from the village a poor peasant woman came
running. She placed her foot upon one rock and then another
until she reached the pinnacle of that crag. With the little
baby in one arm, she came back down and marched through
the crowd among the shouts of praise. As she was going hurriedly through the crowd someone stopped her and said, "How
did you do it? These men who were specialists could not do
it."

She said, "You don't understand, there is a tie between

that baby and me, and the tie is of blood, for I am his mother."

There is a tie between us and every person of the world and it's the tie of blood; the blood of Jesus Christ on the cross which was shed for all. Love like that is dangerous. Even though it could cause us to fall and hurt ourselves, it is the only way to save the infants whether they are infant because of their poverty, because of their sin, or because of their problems; we must go up. And you know something? When you go after another it is always a climb upward—closer to God— for yourself.

3

The Called or the Claimed

(Acts 11:19-26)

There is often a vast difference between what one claims to be and what others know him to be. Often we claim virtues for ourselves on the basis that we ought to possess them; but in reality, we have nothing of the kind. And the truth of the matter is that there is a great tendency for people to believe what others say of us, rather than what we say of ourselves.

Suppose you want some work done and ask me about a particular man who had his name listed in the yellow pages as a carpenter. If I replied, "He *calls* himself a carpenter," with the proper inflection of my voice, you would look elsewhere.

Or, if I were to ask you about a man with *"doctor"* in front of his name for possible surgery for me and you were to say, "Do you prefer lilies or white roses at the service?" I would find another physician.

The fact of the matter is, we are known by our services— our abilities, our traits. By and large, these would accurately describe us. Certainly they would be a more reliable description than we would give ourselves.

The question then comes to us who call ourselves Christians, What would the world call us by merely observing our way of life? Would our *claim* match their *call?*

As we look in this well-known passage in Acts 11:26, we find this worthy sentence, "And the disciples were called Christians first in Antioch." Note that it doesn't say that "they

28

called themselves Christians," but that 'others *called* them that.

If you want not only to claim that you are a Christian but would like the world to call you one as well, I have some suggestions.

Cultivate a Faith That Is Obvious

Illuminating the book of Acts like brilliant stars are phrases that describe the early Christians as people of dynamic faith. You can read phrases, such as "full of the Holy Spirit"; "believing mightily"; "speaking boldly"; "greatly rejoicing"; and galaxies of others that indicate that those first-century disciples never considered the word *timid* and never forgot the word *excited.*

Their faith and commitment to the work of Christ was as obvious as the fact that they were alive. They made the air electric with their joy in Christ.

Why didn't they claim to be Christians? Because everyone knew it. You don't walk up to someone and say, "Hello, I'm a man. What are you?" Nor do you say, "Good morning, I'm wearing a blue jacket." A man doesn't have to call attention to that which is obvious. If a man must announce that he has great faith, he probably has very little faith.

In *Why Revival Tarries,* Leonard Ravenhill quotes Galatians 6:17, "I bear in my body the marks of the Lord Jesus." From this passage he launches into a series of ways by which we can make the fact of our Christianity obvious. He insists that, as I am trying to say, we can be branded in such a way that others shall see us as Christians.

He uses Paul as our example to say that we ought to be *branded by devotion to a task.* When a complete stranger asked if Paul were a Christian (if anyone could have been that much out of touch with the affairs of that day), the Bible doesn't record anyone ever saying, "He claims to be." Paul was too highly devoted to his task for anyone to doubt. His eye was single for the cause of Christ.

Paul was also *branded by humility*. It was obvious to others that Paul was a Christian because of his attitude of complete self-forgetfulness. "What things were gain to me," says Paul, "those things I counted as loss for Christ" (Phil. 3:7).

Mr. Ravenhill continues. Paul was *branded by suffering*. His faith was obvious. He never flinched one single time from his Christian duties, even if it meant a shipwreck, a lashing, a stoning, or whatever. Let the storms break lose, he was ready.

Also, the apostle was *branded by passion*. This burning commitment to live for his Master never ceased its blazing flame until the last pump of that great heart snuffed it out.

Furthermore, Paul was *branded by love*. A faith that is an obvious faith must somewhere be branded with love. Quoting Mr. Ravenhill again, he says Paul loved "the lost, the last, and the least."

When Paul said he bore the marks for Christ, he meant that if he were to take off his coat, on his back you would see cuts and scabs, maybe even fresh blood. We are not called upon now to bear marks of this nature very often, but there ought to be something that communicates our faith to a watching world. Our claims to be Christian should not cause shock to the hearer. Imagine what we could do in our world if it were said about 80 percent of our church members, "My, there is a real Christian!" Do we bear enough "Christian marks" to be *called* one?

Amy Carmichael came near a worldwide need when she prayed, "Give me a love that leads the way; a faith which nothing can dismay."

Called or claimed? Obvious faith?

Have a Contagious Spirit

Second of all, you can determine whether you are a Christian by call or claim not only by an obvious faith but also if you have a contagious spirit. Almost immediately you find those early Christians out mingling and mixing with the people. They had something in their lives called Jesus Christ, and they wanted to live it to the hilt and every place they went—they were Christian. They were devoted, loving, and their lives were set apart for the cause of Christ. Their spirit of enthusiasm, their spirit of love, their spirit of unusual devotion was unexcelled in history. They were ablaze with this newfound cause.

Do you know there is no such thing in this world as an uninfluential Christian? There are not any. I have heard people say, "Well, he just doesn't bear an influence. He just doesn't have an influence." But he does. There is no Christian in the world who is an uninfluential Christian. I know Christians who bear a great influence for Christ. I know some who, as far as the kingdom of God is concerned, it would have been better for the reputation of the church if they had never joined it. Their influence for Christ is negative; it is bad; it is a minus instead of a plus; it is against instead of for. When a person does things only for convenience, only for ease, and only for self-pleasure, he doesn't show that he is committed to anything outside of his own selfish pursuits. He bears an influence, but it is a negative one.

The spirit of the early Christians was contagious. While they were in prayer meetings, and while they were reading their Scriptures, and while they were gathered together, they were preparing to go out and permeate the world. Those early Christians went out into the world and began to witness and all of a sudden the enthusiasm, the vigor, and the vitality of their faith began to flow through the lives of others. Those who once looked on them in ridicule and criticism were bearing the same faith before long and hundreds were filled with the Holy Spirit.

Because their spirit was contagious, it meant something. I was visiting with a church member not too long ago. The husband was gone and I said to the lady, "We certainly have been missing you folks at church. We wish that you would come."

"Oh, I'm sorry, but my husband has an awful time with his heart. It's just an awful thing. He has to rest, and we spend all day Sunday just resting."

I said, "Well, I certainly understand that you would not want to do anything that would interfere with your husband's health. We all must be careful at this point. I suppose that he is retired."

"Oh, no, no, he has a hundred men under him out at the plant and he has to work five days a week."

It's kind of tragic to me that this kind of Christianity exists in our world, in our cities, and in our churches. It's kind of a pitiful thing when a man can risk his heart five days a week in hard labor but cannot risk his heart to sit in an air-conditioned church for thirty minutes to bear a positive witness for Jesus. There is nothing contagious about that kind of Christianity.

I watched the series on television, "The Rise and Fall of The Third Reich." Germany had been one of the great Christian nations of Europe. Lutheranism had the greatest scholars that Christianity has ever had. Yet with all of their preaching, with all of their efforts, something came into the lives of those people and swept them into a world of madness. And the world can never forget the horrible crimes that were committed at Dauchau and Auschwitz. Christianity of that day had grown apathetic. It had grown complacent. Even though great theologians stood before great congregations, the people kept their church within the walls of the building. So when Hitler marched, the few who were strong suddenly faded away. A cause that was damnable began to get more attention than Christianity had for the centuries it had been in Germany.

In our day there are those who fall behind on their pledges because the churches won't send them bills. There are those who, because the churches won't kick them out, stay at home on Sunday night. There are those in our churches who say they believe in prayer but never come to prayer meeting. We have missionary societies which pray and socialize regularly but never really get involved in winning people to firm Christian discipleship. It's no wonder in our world that Christianity is begging for help—that it is gasping for its own life. It is under water trying to breathe through a reed, and church members are on top of the water sticking their fingers in the air hole.

Christianity is dying of suffocation within its own walls. There must come a day when Christians have the Spirit that is not only sweet but also contagious. We can meet in our buildings every day until the world dies and goes to hell. You don't give people a disease they already have. You give Christianity to people who don't have it, who have never known the revolutionary power of Christ. But we quarantine ourselves in the church; we quarantine ourselves into social activity, and the world remains lost.

I went to a revival recently. At least it was called that. I think I've gotten more inspiration from aspirin commercials on television. There was no challenge, no enthusiasm, no dedication. You could have heard the same thing in a social hall.

This kind of Christianity is literally making our churches full of empty pews because the people have empty hearts. We are looking at a world that is not contracting Christianity because we don't have the disease enough for it to be infectious to the lives of others. The early Christians were *called* Christians. They didn't claim to be; their lives were contagious with the spirit of happiness and a glow of enthusiasm for the cause of Christ. You don't have to claim the obvious.

Arnold Toynbee said, "Apathy can only be overcome by enthusiasm. And enthusiasm can only come by two things, an ideal taking the imagination by storm and some pragmatic way into which that idea may be implemented." I can think of no greater problem in the church than apathy. But it's only going to be overcome by an enthusiasm and by a vitality that will help a seeking world find Christ. Let's march forward and win this world for Christ.

One of our deacons and I were out visiting some time ago. "Wouldn't it be wonderful if we had ten men doing what we are doing every week; just ten men witnessing for Christ every week," I said. What we could do for our world!

When Jesus said, "Ye are the salt of the earth," I don't really know what he meant, but I like to think that he meant when a person tastes of our lives that, as salt causes thirst, our lives for Christ will cause a world to be thirsty for more—more of the water of life. How thirsty do you make a watching world? How contagious is your spirit? How enthusiastic are you for the cause of Jesus Christ?

Have Power with a Purpose

The New Testament Christians really had something. They didn't participate in the organizations because the pastor would visit them if they didn't. They did not go to church because it was the thing to do. They had a purpose. They had a reason. They believed in something. Their purpose was that, through their lives, through their living, and through their commitment to a cause, the world might see in them what Christ is all about. They believed with all of their heart and with all of their life.

Why? Because they were closer to Christ than we are. Many of those people had seen his resurrection. They had seen him die on the cross. They had seen him after his resurrection. Some of them had literally stood on the ground and watched Christ ascend into heaven.

Sometimes I think the very reason you and I are not committed is because we don't believe. We must rethink our belief in Christ, his infallible Word, his lordship over our lives, and on bowed knees pray, "Dear Jesus, remind me of what thou has done, what thou art doing, and what thou shalt do." If we do that, we will arise different people with new power and purpose. If we really believe, could we possibly not have power?

Back to the series on television, "The Rise and the Fall of The Third Reich." I think Nazism had some things that we need. Hitler believed that there ought to be a people that is above all. I agree with him. I wish every Christian believed that. I wish we all were committed enough to say, "I believe that everyone ought to be a Christian. I want to march across this globe, not with cruel arms and bloody swords, but with the message of God's redeeming love." Yes, what a thought— a world of twice-born men.

We will have to have another quality those Germans had. We will have to believe that the purpose is more important than the person. The army teaches that the mission is more important than the men. It ought to be so in the church. Therefore, a person doesn't say, "I'm too tired." "I don't want to." "I haven't got the time." But he does say, "Master, I will follow thee."

How many of us have a purpose or goal for Christ? How many of us have put God in our calendar? What have you done for the Lord? What have you done for the Lord this week? Many of us have plans for next week and next month and next year, but what do we have for God next year? Have you put him in your date book? Have you put him in your calendar?

The large, beautiful tree was finally cut in the forest. It was put in the stream with the others. On the way to the sawmill, this mighty redwood drifted aside from the other logs. Finally, after some weeks, the log drifted into the ocean. A seaman on a small vessel approaching the large mass, which once could have been used to build a mighty structure, yelled, "Wait a moment, danger ahead, danger ahead!" The captain went to the front of the boat and looked over and said, "Full speed ahead—it is just driftwood."

God has blessed some of us in great ways. He has given us good personalities and good minds. Yet when he takes us from the forest of sin and wants to make something of which he can build a great kingdom upon, we drift aside into the sea of idleness. Finally the indictment of the world is not "Christian" but "driftwood," drifting along following the path of least resistance.

Do you have to *claim* to be a Christian or could someone *call* you one? Let's have a faith that is obvious, a spirit that is contagious, and a purposeful life with power from above.

4

Pitifully Pleasing or Pleasantly Powerful

(Acts 12)

With forty-five million aspirin sold each day, twenty million sleeping pills consumed each evening, forty million tranquilizer prescriptions filled every year, and with mounting reports of an unequalled number of suicides, is it any wonder that W. H. Auden has called this "the age of anxiety"? Isn't it strange that our troubles seem to grow with every increase of our material blessings?

No simple solution is forthcoming. However, I feel that one of our deep-rooted problems is our lack of firm commitment to one high and lofty set of principles. Anxiety is caused by this tug and pull of life with no solid home base where a person can say, "Here I stand."

Our age is trying to please style, contemporary expectations, and greater social pressures to conform more than ever before in our nation's history. Some people are like pawns being moved backward and forward and sideways according to the player who holds them. The inevitable result of this crazy and senseless desire to please is anxiety.

Well, a man by the name of Herod, long years ago, decided it was important to please certain groups without thought of its consequences to others. Yet, while Herod was pitifully trying to please, he was never pleasant because his desire to please was not built on good reason.

The young Christian church that he opposed, pleasant with their noble and righteous cause and powerful with the strength of their God, moved forward caring only to please their Master.

Acts 12 offers some principles which can help in seeking a pleasant life by pleasing the right One. With this discovery, anxiety will drown in a sea of divine purpose.

Pleasing Is Not Always a Virtue

To be pleasing is not always a virtue. To give in, to abide by, to undertake to oblige, to see that what is requested is done, is not always a good practice. But think of Herod. You've heard of Herod before. You've heard of Herod the Great, who killed all of the children in the days of Jesus. Well, he was this man's grandfather. You've heard of Herod Antipas who arrested John the Baptist and had him beheaded. This Herod was the nephew of that Herod. They were all related both in blood and lack of principles. They all had tendencies toward cruelty and following the group.

Acts 12:3 makes a revealing statement about Herod the king. This Herod had killed a great and noble man by the name of James, one of the great stalwart, intellectual, leaders of the church. Herod saw that when he killed James that the Jews were pleased. So he thought if it made the Jews happy to kill James, how much happier would it make them to kill Peter—a man full of passion and love for the cause of Christ.

Herod had Peter arrested and thrown in prison. Iron chains were placed upon Peter's wrists and a guard was stationed on each side. Besides those guards, sixteen others had to guard Simon Peter. This was an unusually great number of guards. Well, Peter was a big, husky man, and the guards probably questioned their power up beside Peter's great body and courageous personality. But I think more than that, Herod even with all of his harassing, with all of his sin, with all of his evil, began to wonder, Now, just how strong am I up against this man's God?

This man's action was based upon one solitary reason—it

pleased the Jews. Herod, in the beginning of his reign, had trouble after trouble, difficulty piled upon difficulty, and discord stacked upon discord. He got to the point of frustration and said, "I will do anything to make me more appealing to the people who keep me in office—I will please them."

Isn't it tragic that a man will kill; that a man will put another man in prison; that a man will forget about ideals, virtues, honesty, and moral judgment on the basis that he's got to please some particular group of people? Isn't that a tragic hour? And yet, we are in the same situation today. How about the church which recently voted to cancel Sunday night meetings? Their excuse was, "Well, the people just didn't want it." So to please those halfhearted souls who can't take the Lord but one hour a week, they cancelled meetings on Sunday night.

Or, how about the preacher who gave the invocation at the dedication of a brewery in Fort Worth, Texas? When somebody asked him, "Why did you pray for the dedication of a brewery?" He said, "Well, I thought it would please the community if I did so." Or, how about the young girl who goes too far in giving her charms to an aggressive young man and after reaping the rewards of that tragedy, her only reply was, "Well, that's what it took to please him."

Isn't it a sad day when we base our judgments upon pleasing particular people and groups and not upon what is right and what is good and what is morally correct? I'm sometimes disgruntled at how far some people will go to be in style. I sometimes think that if it became popular in Paris, London, New York, or Dallas, simply to wear a collar and nothing else, that's exactly what some people would wear. No matter how short the skirt; no matter how sordid the business parties; no matter how strong the beverage; no matter how damaging the literature; the sad conclusion of many is a misdirected, "I've got to please."

You and I must have better judgment for ourselves than

just that which pleases man-made standards. Isn't there some kind of divine standard upon which we ought to base our lives and our words and our actions? God help us not to be little Herods who run around saying, "Well, I've got to do this because it pleases the Jews; it pleases the boys; it pleases the girls; it pleases the fad, it pleases the in-group." Let us get away from this effort to please people while God is completely forgotten. Are you just the kind of pitiful person who has no real basis upon which to stand, your life is governed instead by his demands, her demands, or this one's demands? How tragic!

Pleasing is not always a virtue. Isn't it a sad thing how far people will go just to please? I had an acquaintance who managed a tire store in Dallas. A customer came in one day and I heard my friend tell so many lies to the man, I was shocked that a friend of mine would do that. He told one lie after another and I said, "Ron, what in the world is wrong with you? I knew better than what you were telling the man." Do you know what he said? "The public expects you to lie to them." He believed it—anything to please, right or wrong.

What about the movie industry? Someone in theological circles recently approached the movie industry and said, "Why are you producing such filth?" Do you know what they said? "That's what the public wants." Their whole idea was expediency, money, and selling the product irrespective of a moral standard upon which a man's actions ought to be based. Have we lost our minds and consciences?

I think of those unfortunate models who are forced to wear things that you should wear only in your own bedroom. They must expose themselves to the world because it's the style. Should not one of those models, even though it is her livelihood, stand up and say, "I'm sorry, I will not wear it"?

Shouldn't there be some things that a person belonging to Jesus Christ will not do just to please? The Jews, whom Herod was trying to please, were against the work of Christ.

Isn't it a shame that we often please people who are antichurch more than we please Jesus who died and shed his blood that we might have a church in the first place? We are guilty of trying to please the wrong people.

There is certainly no better illustration of this truth than the Old Testament drama of Samson. While Samson was concerned only with pleasing God, he had power unequalled. But when he became concerned with pleasing the requests of someone named Delilah, he lost his power, his purpose, and inevitably his life. You can't serve God and mammon.

Pleasing God—Life's Noblest Virtue

When Peter went to prison, God's people got down on their knees. Peter went behind bars and Peter's friends were behind the altar. When Peter needed an angel, the people prayed that God's angels would come. They decided that whatever Herod did, they would pray.

Peter was in prison and the angel came. The chains dropped from Peter's hands. The angel told Peter to put on his sandals. Peter had not planned to go any place. He didn't really know the angel was going to come. He had his shoes off, ready to spend the night. After Peter fastened his sandals, he and the angel went off together. Peter thought he was having a dream; but when he discovered himself free, he knew it was real. Those sixteen soldiers, plus the two beside Peter, never saw the angel. But he came and delivered Peter from the prison.

Verse 10 says, "When they were past the first and the second ward, they came unto the iron gate that leadeth unto the city; which opened to them of his own accord: and they went out, and passed on through one street; and forthwith the angel departed from him." As they were coming up to the gate, Peter might have nudged the angel a little bit and said, "Brother Angel, I'm a little concerned with that iron gate that we are going to have to go through to get out of this trouble." I doubt if the angel said anything because Peter was always the one who was able to see problems before they arose anyway. As they came close enough for their noses to touch that cold iron, the gate swung open, and they marched through. I can imagine that Peter was amazed and shocked and that his heart began to beat a little faster.

When we try to do life's noblest virtue by pleasing God, there will be iron gates. I've had them in my life to such an extent that I've said to myself in my little faith, How will this ever come out? A cliff isn't as hard to climb as it looked like it would be when you were a mile away. No mountain is quite as steep as it appeared two or three hundred yards back, when you looked at it and dreaded the task that was yours.

Have you ever tried to please God and suddenly an iron gate was shut tight? You thought to yourself, How am I ever going to get through? But as you marched in faith, believing God, taking him at his word, the gate miraculously opened. The mistake you and I often make is that we decide too early that God is not going to open the gate, and we give up. We stop short of the promises, the love, and the fulfillment that he has, instead of going right to the point where the testing of our faith is really placed on the balance.

Isn't it surprising that the angel left Peter? But that's the way life is. How many spiritual mountaintops and high points are there in life? It seems that God cannot be any closer. The angel of the Lord is with you and the gates are opening up all along the way. Momentarily, the majestic presence of God seems to leave you. You just don't feel as close to him as you used to. You just don't feel as dynamic for Christ as you once did.

"And forthwith the angel departed from him" (12:10). There was still another door. There was still another gate; yet, the angel left. "And as Peter knocked at the door of the gate, a damsel came to hearken, named Rhoda" (v. 13). Now isn't that strange that the Lord would do Peter that way? He got him through one gate, but there was still another gate and the angel was gone.

Do you know why the angel left Peter? Because God refuses to do things for us that we can do for ourselves. Peter did not have the power to open that iron gate, but he had the power to knock on a door. The angel of God knew that on the other side of that door was help. This might also indicate that God often refuses to do for some in need, what others could do for them.

Look at Rhoda! Bless her heart. She had more emotion than she had sense. Do you know anybody like that—more heart than brains? Sometimes I prefer that though over more brains than heart. But anyway, Rhoda came to the door and saw Peter. She might have thought to herself, Oh, wonderful, wonderful, wonderful, how wonderful a thing this is. She began to jump up and shout as only a girl could do. She is just overwhelmed. She ran and left Peter behind the door and told the others. They told her, "You're mad. We're praying for Peter—don't bother us." Rhoda was so happy that God had worked his salvation that she didn't let Peter in "for gladness."

Did you ever know anybody like that? Some people can sing, "Oh, How I Love Jesus." They can sing, "Rescue the Perishing." They can sing lustily on Sunday morning. They can shout "glory to God" on Sunday evening. Yet, while shouting the praises of God, they forget what really pleases God. They leave the man on the outside. They get excited about what God can do but never do anything that God needs for them to do. And this was Rhoda's problem. She believed she saw a miracle, but in her selfish excitement, she forgot about the outsider who needed in.

Are you guilty of rejoicing for what Jesus has done for you and of forgetting to open the door for someone else to come in? Rhoda had probably been very good at praying for Peter, but she completely failed in opening the door. Many of us are good at caring long distance, but when pleasing God demands our opening the door to whoever knocks, we had rather just sing and shout.

In doing God's will, there are just some gates we must open. He may provide the ones wanting in, but we must be his hands to turn the knob. "But Peter continued knocking" (v. 16)! We've never seen this aspect of Peter before. Impulsive, passionate, hot-tempered Peter was patient. That's what you're going to have to do on the outside trying to come in to God's will. Keep on knocking. You will need to pray, "Lord, I don't know if the door is ever going to open, but if you'll give me strength, I'll keep on knocking."

At a fair some time ago, a miniature mine was shown. The owner drove a tunnel a mile long through the strata he thought contained gold. He spent one-hundred thousand dollars on it and in a year and a half failed to find gold. Another company drove the tunnel a yard further and struck the ore. Three more feet.

Sometimes pleasing God seems an impossible task, but keep knocking. Peter did. Keep knocking lost man, some of us will wake up and tell you how to be saved. We'll quit shouting "Jesus saves" and start doing something about it. Keep knocking. Keep going, Christian; keep going, preacher, don't give up; keep knocking. There's salvation, there's hope, there's comfort—all behind the door. Keep knocking.

Never Doubt the Power of
People Who Please God

Peter was dedicated to pleasing the Lord. Never doubt the power of people who please God. Herod had persecuted so mercilessly these people called Christians; yet when the truth was known, they were far ahead of Herod. James had been killed. Peter had been put into the prison.

What happened to Herod? Josephus tells what happened to Herod. Herod marched out in that great arena with a silver suit on and the people saw the sun glistening on that silver and began to shout, "He is God, he is God." Herod took credit for being God and the angel of the Lord struck him and the worms began to eat his body as he died. Herod the man who wanted to please the Jews, the man who wanted to please the world was dead. Poor Herod was dead.

"But the word of God grew and multiplied" (Acts 12:24). What can prayer do against a man in prison? It can free him. What can a prayer do for a man who is lost? It can save him. What can prayer do for a Christian who is backslidden? It can bring him back to church. While we are praying, God is working.

Where do you find yourself? Pitifully trying to please the world and its standards? Are you a Herod? Are you the kind of person who tries to please but pitifully is unhappy? You see, Herod was pleasing, but he wasn't very pleasant. These Christians pleasing God became powerful enough to shake a jail down. Herod died and the Word of God continued. Even a church, at times, begins to want to please the world instead of God. Do you know why verse 24 says, "the word of God grew and multiplied"? The early church was not concerned with pleasing worldly men; it was concerned with needy people; it was concerned with God; it was concerned with prayer; it was concerned with faith. Whatever else we have to give up in our churches, let us not give up our faith, our prayer, and our love for God. Let us never do it. For we must never doubt the power of a life that pleases God. As long as the church pleases man she is worthless; but as long as she pleases God—the gates of hell shall never prevail against her.

5

Crosses Make Good Crusaders

(Acts 13:1-3)

The truth that interest is in direct proportion to investment has been proven a thousand times over. That which has cost a man something has its magnetic means of drawing him close.

The young man who has spent months working on his old jalopy is more proud of it than if someone had given it to him in the condition that he now has it. The young lady enjoys wearing a garment that took tedious hours of painstaking labor.

Parenthood is certainly an appropriate example of this truth. A mother naturally loves her child in a special way. Why shouldn't she? She went through the pregnancy, pains of labor, and birth for her child. Her dawn-to-dark labor are done for her child. And of the father, the feelings are no less. His child has made greater demands on his time, means, and energies.

When it comes to meaning something for Jesus and having him and his marvelous work mean something to you, the principle is epitomized. No man has ever meant much to the program of Christ unless he has, at some time or another, borne a cross for his Lord.

In Acts 13:1-3, we read the names of the men who were prophets and teachers in Antioch. It is a startling fact that each of these men had paid a price and borne a cross in a genuine sense to become a follower of Christ. There were, of course, hundreds of other disciples, but the ones who really cared enough to be crusaders and risk the dangers of rough seas and rugged terrain, and who really became the powder for the cannon of the early work, had been these who had let following Christ cost them something. They had invested too much to be just nominal stragglers.

Let us note each of these men and the cross he bore to belong to Christ and see the irrefutable truth that *crosses make good crusaders.*

Manaen—The Cross of the Wrong Friends

Look, if you will, at this man Manaen. Here is a man of whom I knew absolutely nothing. In fact, as I studied, I will have to confess honestly that I didn't remember anything ever having been said about the man, Manaen. If anybody had asked me if the word, *Manaen,* was in the Bible—I would have probably answered, "Not to my knowledge." But here he is, this man that had been relegated to obscurity; this man of whom Christianity had beforehand said absolutely nothing; this man of whom a seminary graduate had never heard. This man about whom scholars seldom write; this man that is less than frequently the theme of somebody's sermon, or any Sunday School teacher's devotional thought, is placed all of a sudden as one of the most prominent men in the work of the early church. He is taken from a place of obscurity and catapulted into the national Christian spotlight. Why? Because he, along with Paul and Barnabas, was one of five men who volunteered, out of hundreds and thousands of others, to be involved in the initial missionary work of the church. Manaen, the insignificant man, gave up security to be a pioneer for this Galilean who had taken his heart by storm.

What we know about the man is limited but interesting. It was a custom in biblical days that when a young prince was born, he was to pick a playmate from the peasants and the common people. The king's young son could pick anybody that he wanted. That person came to live with him in the palace and in the courtroom. It so happened that when King

Herod was born to the older Herod, he chose a little boy by the name of Manaen. Manaen came to live with young Prince Herod and they grew together as young boys, as teenagers, and as men.

Close as they were, loving as they were, as binding as that friendship came to be, as young Prince Herod and little peasant Manaen grew up together—becoming as brothers in the court of his father, Herod—something happened when manhood came that put a strain on that relationship.

Imagine what young Manaen must have seen living in the court of Herod. He heard all of the words that were spoken about the man called Jesus. He may have been there when Christ stood before Herod and had witnessed the illegal court proceedings.

Manaen, as a grown man, disagreed (I suppose) with all that Herod was doing and had to face a fact. The fact was this. From a boy he was raised in the court with the young prince. Now here Prince Herod is the king of this great nation, but he wholly disagreed with all for which his adopted brother stood.

The cross Manaen had to bear was this. He had to choose over royal entanglements and friendships for the cause of Jesus Christ, whom he knew to be wonderful, loving, powerful, good, wholesome, and right. He made his decision and became one of the first missionary supporters the church ever had. How he ever came to know the Savior, we're not really sure. He had to bear a cross to follow him, we do know for certain.

No man ever amounts to anything for Jesus unless he has given up something for Jesus. And this man looked at all of the advantages of royalty. He looked at his friend, Herod, and thought to himself, What am I going to do?

He chose Christ. He chose the path of the Lord. And because of his costly Christianity, when in that company of people the question was asked, "Who will go?" Manaen, who had been among the enemies of Christ, who had been around a court that was dedicated to the destruction of Christ, now said, "I will follow Jesus."

There are some people in the world who need to bear crosses like that. There are some in our world who have not yet seen the importance of the right company in life. We need to get rid of ideas like the one a young girl expressed to me as I tried to talk her out of marrying a young man. "Preacher, I know that he drinks and I know that he cusses. I know that he's loose with the women, but I love him." She didn't realize that there comes a time to follow Christ fully. The decision is between what you would like and what you know you must do.

Some people won't bear that cross. There are some who say, "My boss told me that unless I go to that New Year's party, unless I tell the filthy jokes and unless I hold the cocktail glass, I won't get the promotion that is coming up." So what happens? They stay there in the group dedicated against Christ and never amount to anything for the Lord because they will not bear the cross. The only way anyone will ever become a crusader, the only way anyone will ever become a real stalwart soldier for Christ, is to be willing with all of his heart and soul to bear his cross.

Your cross may not be my cross, and my cross may not be yours; but you have one and I have one. Bearing it will help make us Christlike.

Manaen was willing to bear that cross of friendship, and don't you know that it hurt him? You can imagine that Herod said to him, "Manaen, come into my chamber. Is it true that you're going to follow that nasty Nazarene? Could it be true, Manaen, that the boy I picked out when I was just a boy, to belong to me and to be my playmate, could turn his back on me now? I fed you; I clothed you; and you had every privilege of royalty, and you're going to follow that filthy carpenter!"

His courageous answer sounded against the columns of that court when he said, "Yes."

Some of you, right this moment, are faced with this very question. You are faced with whether it ought to be others or Christ. Some of you have not yet had enough courage to say, "It ought to be Christ in my life above everything." You're not willing to sever relations with some of those people and places which would drag you down. You are not willing to bear that cross. This was the cross Manaen had to bear. This is the cross you must bear to really be significant in the Lord's work.

Barnabas—The Cross of Financial Liberality

Here is a man of whom we have heard. His name is Barnabas. "Now there were in the church that was at Antioch certain prophets and teachers; as Barnabas" (v. 1).

What cross did he have to bear? When he became a Christian, he confessed that he didn't have any talents. He couldn't preach; he was not eloquent. He was just a little bit like Joseph of Arimathea. He didn't know what he could do, but he knew that, above all things in this world, he loved Jesus and his work with all of his heart.

There came a financial crisis in the church. Barnabas sold all that he had and gave to the work of that early church. It's a dramatic story of how Barnabas, who wasn't doing much for Christ, all of a sudden became prominent in the kingdom. He gave up his wealth and bore the cross of financial sacrifice in order to be on the front line for Jesus Christ. He, along with Manean, became a powerful missionary force of the church. By bearing a cross, he became a crusader as one of the church's first missionaries. What a dramatic story!

I've never known in my life one man or woman in the church that was faithful, loving, devoted, soul-concerned and dedicated to the work of Christ who would not bear the cross (is it really a cross?) of giving. Many of you will never be crusaders for Christ and won't really mean much to the church because, when it comes to giving money, you hold back.

During the invitation you sing, "I Surrender All." You sing at other times, "Have Thine Own Way," but unlike Barnabas you are afraid to bear this cross on your shoulder of financial fairness with Jesus Christ and his work. Because you give 5 percent instead of 10 percent you struggle along as a mediocre Christian and never mean much to the church and to God's work. How many of you have been afraid to bear that cross? You've not been a crusader because there's a cross that you've not borne. Those that bear a cross also wear a crown.

It would be a sad thing sometimes to look on church records and see people the Lord has blessed with extraordinary incomes, who are so stingy and selfish with God's blessings. If people would pick up the cross of financial fairness with the Lord and bear it as Barnabas did, the church could meet every one of its material needs.

Jesus said, "Where your treasure is, there will your heart be also" (Matt. 6:21). Now, he didn't say if you give your heart to God that he'll get your money. He said just the opposite. Jesus indicated, that if you'll give him your money, the heart will take care of itself. That's true. If a man is giving of his means to the Lord, he will have a greater interest in every avenue of the church's ministry.

The Old Testament prophet asked, "Will a man rob God?" And if those people under law gave 10 percent, how much more should we give under grace and twentieth-century blessings.

I've had people say to me, "Preacher, don't preach on tithing. I just give a little bit as it comes in." "I just can't know how much I'm going to give." But they know about the house payment, the car payment, the water bill, the gas bill, the clothes bill. But when it comes to the work of the church—it is left to chance, it's left to circumstance, it's left to maybes and ifs.

If you are not a tither or giver and you begin to be one, I promise that you'll love the church like you've never loved it before. You'll feel like you belong to it. You'll have a better relationship with its workers and love God's kingdom more because where your investment is, there is where you will inevitably find your highest interest.

A committee at a church was trying to go into a building program over a period of three years. They asked the people to make a pledge over that length of time. A poor washwoman belonged to the church. She sent in her card with a commitment of $468.00 over a period of three years. The pastor and deacons just couldn't believe it, and they went to see her. They said to her, "We know that you love the church and the work, but you cannot give $468.00 in three years. All you do is wash clothes to make your living."

She replied, "No, I figured it up. I wash three places a day, but I've got another place I can wash. I've turned it down because I've been too tired, but I've decided to do it for three years and I'm going to give that extra $3.00 a day for three years to the building program." She continued, "Don't cheat me of this privilege." Instead of doing three washes a day in the neighborhood, she took four, and she called the fourth wash "the Lord's wash."

There is much more that we can do. For those of you who are robbing and stealing from God's pockets, pray today, husband and wife together, and say, "What can we do to be more involved in the work of the church?" When you tithe and give of your means, you become a better church member in every way.

I don't believe any Christian, if Christ were to walk into the church, would push him to the floor hoping to break his legs. No, you would fall in humble reverence and obedience, and as Mary fell at his feet; you would begin to worship. Yet, there are people in churches who are crippling Christ by their stinginess and selfishness and by their inconsideration toward the needs of Christ's kingdom. I've never liked anybody to ride in a boat and not paddle, but some do that in a church. "Let others give it." "Let others support it." "I'll just enjoy it." "I don't want to do anything to help it along." "I'll just take." "I'll just receive." "I won't give." Some are saying this—the records prove it.

Saul—The Cross of Personal Forgetfulness

"And there was a man by the name of Saul." We all know about this man Saul who was converted on the road to Damascus—this man of unusual greatness in mind and in character, although initially a murderer and an enemy of the church. He said yes to Christ and took the ridicule of the world upon him. But here is Paul, a crusader, one of the first missionaries of the church, and he had to bear a cross to be one.

He had to give up most of the security of his Roman citizenship. He had to relinquish all of the wonderful opportunities that came his way as an important man in religious government. But he did give it up, willing to do so because he knew that, unless he was willing to bear a cross for Christ, he would never mean anything for him in the days ahead. He chose to bear the cross of giving up that which was to his advantage. Some of us won't bear that cross.

When I was in Hawaii for a summer, a church called a pastor from the mainland. They received a phone call later in the summer that he had decided not to come. The chairman of the pulpit committee said, "Oh, I'm sorry, we thought that you told us it was the Lord's will that you come. We were looking forward to it so much."

The preacher answered, "Well, it is the Lord's will, and I really feel like we would have a great ministry together, but we checked into moving my wife's antique furniture, and it will just cost too much to move it and she's afraid it will get scarred. You just can't replace stuff like that anymore."

So this man, "called" of God, turned down a place where

he, himself, admitted that God wanted him to go, because his wife was afraid of moving the antique furniture.

He wasn't any crusader for Christ. He wasn't really on fire. He didn't really mean much to God's work. He was floating along with the crowd unwilling to bear a cross.

He was unlike Paul, who was willing to turn his back on earthly possessions and say, "I'll pick up my cross." And it was Paul who said, "But God forbid that I should glory, save in the cross of our Lord Jesus Christ" (Gal. 6:14). He said again, "I determine not to know any thing among you, save Jesus Christ, and him crucified" (1 Cor. 2:2).

Have you failed to really be involved in Christ and his work? Is there some comfort, some ease, some habit that you're afraid to give up? Unless you give it up, you won't amount to much for Christ. You won't ever be a bona fide missionary. You won't be out there where the going is rough and where the test of discipleship is demanded. You'll never be there. Paul certainly epitomizes the truth.

Niger—The Cross of Calvary

Ah, the story of this man is beautiful to me. This is a moving story. Sometimes when you write you get so excited your mind wants your pen to move faster than it can. Such is the case here.

Here is a man by the name of Niger, or Simon. Do you know who he was? Some scholars feel that this man is Simon of Cyrene, the man who was standing in the crowd when the procession with Jesus carrying the cross came by. The soldiers saw this black man from Cyrene, (the northern part of Africa) and jerked him out from the crowd and said, "You take this man's cross, he's too weak to carry it." Simon may have bitterly detested what the Roman soldier made him do, but he put his back under that cross and carried it to the crest of Calvary.

And now, he was a volunteer worker for the Lord, eagerly

ready to bear the cross again. Isn't that an intriguing story? This man became a crusader. This man became a missionary. He became a sacrifice upon the altar of service. Only a few days before, he had been jerked up from the mocking crowd and, out of fear for his life, reluctantly bore the cross. Afterwards he carried it joyfully.

When volunteers were requested to be the first missionaries, this black man remembered looking into the face of Jesus on Calvary and responded with an eager, "I'll go. I'll tell others what he did on the cross." The man who helped Jesus carry his cross, volunteered to be one of the first missionaries.

I might bear a cross here and there like Manean and Barnabas and Paul, but do you know that I don't bear the cross of Calvary enough? How long has it been since you've been to the cross? How long has it been since you've been to Calvary?

Niger of Cyrene was on the front line for Christ because he may have watched those nails being driven through Jesus' hands; perhaps he watched that crown of thorns placed upon that precious brow; he heard him cry, "It is finished." This man saw every lash of the whip and heard every cruel word of the crowd and Roman soldiers. His cross-bearing convinced him of his need for Christ.

How many times lately have you seen the blood? How long has it been since you've seen him there on the cross? How long has it been since you've heard the words, "Father forgive them; for they know not what they do." How long has it been since you've said, "Jesus Christ, who am I that you should die for me in such a way as this?" How long has it been since you've been to Golgotha's rugged peak?

Until we bear the cross of Calvary, we won't mean much for the Lord. I don't see how a man can be mediocre or a half-day Sunday worshiper. He needs to go to Calvary every now and then. This man that had seen the sweat and blood dripping from Christ's riddled body had to say, "Yes, I will go."

The reason some of our churches are so dead and dried up and worthless to the kingdom of God is because some people know about everything in the world *except* Calvary. My friend, if you go to the cross, you come back different. For here is the Son of God, without a sin in his life who gave himself and became sin for us. Choirs sing, "Must Jesus bear the cross alone, and all the world go free?" If you have seen the blood that washes away every tear; that meets every problem; that answers every question; that comes to grips with every difficulty; you cannot any longer be mediocre for our Christ. Isn't that a beautiful story? The man that carried the cross became the crusader.

Let me tell you of Ronald Merideth, who played the part of Christ in "The Passion." After he carried the cross across the stage one time, a teenage boy rushed upon the stage, knelt down upon the floor of that stage, put his shoulder under the cross, and surprisingly he couldn't stand up with it. Ronald Merideth began to laugh.

The boy said, "I thought this would be made of cardboard or balsa wood. I thought it wouldn't be heavy and I could carry it." Said he, "Why in the world do you have such a heavy cross if you're just in a play?"

Ronald Merideth looked at that young man and said, "I discovered that I cannot look like the Christ unless I really bear his cross."

How much do you look like Christ—not much if you are unwilling to bear a cross. Those who pay a price to be a follower of Christ usually make the greatest contribution to the kingdom's work. Crosses do indeed make good crusaders.

6
Prescription or Dosage

(Acts 13:42-52)

If the church has a great need today, it is not the need to find a new prescription for its ills. Rather, it needs to take a bigger dose of its original medicine. If the church neglects its command to preach the gospel and win people to Christ, no amount of medicine will do any good. No change in approach will help. All compromising will be foolish. The church's weak condition today is not, therefore, due to its hanging on to some antiquated beliefs. It is due to the fact that the church has forsaken those truths that once made her a strong and mighty force. We don't need to change the prescription, but the dosage.

This corny story illustrates the point I am trying to make. A doctor told a fellow to take three pills home and if he could keep them on his stomach over night, he would be well in the morning. The fellow came back and said, "I don't think I will ever get well. I put the pills on my stomach, but everytime I roll over, they fall off."

The church has been much like this uninformed patient. The prescription from God's Word is still the answer, but we are not taking it internally like we should. We don't want it to really penetrate us and become a part of us. Frankly, some people get so use to their sick condition, they don't care much about changing.

Our need is not to change the prescription, but to change the dosage. When Paul preached his first sermon in Antioch of Pisidia, as recorded in Acts 13, he chose to preach the gospel of Jesus. He was committed to preaching the truth. Paul was convinced that the only hope for the world's salvation was to preach Jesus.

Like Paul, we are faced with the possibility of changing the prescription or the dosage. When faced even with a house full of skeptics, Paul chose to preach the unadulterated truth of God's Word. Pity the preacher who decides otherwise. Let's look fully at this unfolding drama more closely.

When a Strong Enough Dosage of the Gospel Is Taken, There Will Inevitably Be a Reaction

Do you know what a healing medicine is? The only healing medicine is a killing one. Before a medicine can be any good at all, it must cause a death. Medicine must kill the bacteria, the germ, that is present. In order for a sick person to get well, he must take medicine that reacts and kills something. A good illustration of this is what my mother used to say when putting alcohol on a cut, "If it burns, it means it is doing good." Often you shall discover that this is true in life, especially with the gospel. When the gospel of Jesus Christ is preached and listened to, it is impossible for everybody to like it.

Paul began to preach the gospel of Christ and traced the history of the Jewish nation way back to when God adopted them and said, "I will be your God, and you shall be my people" (Lev. 26:12). He told those Jews that the same Jesus whom they had rejected was related to the great Hebrew people of which they also were related. Jesus crucified is the Messiah. Jesus is the resurrected King. Most of the Jews couldn't take that.

Now there are some things Paul could have preached on and everybody would have liked it. Paul could not have preached the gospel and had universal acceptance with it. There is always a reaction; there is always a conflict when the gospel is preached. Notice how many contrasting reactions there were. "They [the Jews] were filled with envy" (v. 45) but the Gentiles "were glad" (v. 48). Some contradicted, others glorified God. Some blasphemed. Others believed. Why is this so? It's so because it seems impossible that the gospel of Jesus can be preached unless there are contrasting reactions.

In dealing with matters of the soul, the heart, and eternity, the message has to cause reaction within the lives of people. There seems to be a correlation between disturbance and acceptance, magnetism to the cause and repulsion from the cause, strong adherence and bitter rejection. For some reason, it is almost impossible to have a strong band of crusaders without a large band of opponents. For when the message is given with the hot zeal fervent enough to demand the hearts of good men, the friends of evil are going to be disturbed. The weak, apologetic appeal does not get much attention from either side. The option seems to be between speaking a strong word for right to rally its supporters to renewed vigor and upset those who are sin-controlled, noncommittal, sterile, compromising words which leave those who could be challenged to great service, lifeless and frustrated.

Paul had that choice. As Paul walked to the rostrum and looked out over those Jews, he said to himself, I can talk about the greatness of Abraham. I can talk about the wonderful work of Moses. I can talk about the great things God did at the Red Sea, the manna from Heaven, the water from the rock.

Paul thought deeper, Am I here to let everybody go away saying, "What a nice fellow Paul is"? Or am I here to say, "Jesus Christ died on the cross and was resurrected, and you are lost without him and you can be saved"? Preachers today have the same decision to make that Paul had. They can either preach the truth and get the job done and rally people who would do good around the cause of Jesus Christ and go forward, or they can preach nothing at all and let everybody be mediocre. Paul had the choice and he made it—to preach the full gospel of Christ.

There just isn't any way in the world you can get crusaders without getting opponents. Now you can get people who stand by, you can get spectators, but you cannot get crusaders with hearts afire without getting opponents. There's no way in the world.

I remember saying to a friend of mine in school that I considered a little fanatic, "George, aren't you a little upset that you don't have as many friends as others have, that some people don't like you, that they're talking about some of the things you believe?"

He said, "Bailey, I would really be upset if people did not become disturbed at what I believe." I think he had a point. For when the gospel of Jesus Christ is preached and it's lived to its fullest, it inevitably has to cause some people anger.

Some people don't like preachers. Some people don't like good Christians. Good Christians make them see what rotten people they are. This is why some students get mad when a young boy comes to school with a New Testament in his pocket. This is what makes young girls unhappy when one girl among many of them lives a better moral life. They respect her, yet she bothers them because they know they ought to be just like her, but they don't have enough Christian courage to do it.

There just isn't any way to live a great Christian life unless you alienate some people. You have to make your choice—living all the way for Jesus Christ, leading others to him or living so mediocre for Christ you'll try to be both a friend of the devil and a friend of God.

A church called a preacher who wasn't known for his great preaching. It was an affluent church, full of rich people. The preacher sat down with the deacons and said, "I don't understand why you want me. I can't preach, I can't do anything. Why did you call me?"

The deacons said, "Well, Preacher, the pulpit committee told us that you were not likely to draw any people to the church, and we just hate a crowded church."

So they got their man. As one lady told her preacher, "I never did like a preacher who really preached. You are really my type." Now that way, you might keep everybody happy.

When the gospel of Jesus Christ is preached and lived, it is going to cause trouble. Let a law enforcement officer do his job; he's going to have trouble. If he wants to stand aside and let the people commit crimes, rob banks, commit immoral acts, murder, he can be friends with all. But when you become easy with the rats, you become friends with the rats. We had better stick with the gospel as Paul preached it.

A great preacher said one day he would die and a minister would stand over him and say, "Oh, brother so and so never had an enemy in his life. Brother so and so never made an enemy." That great preacher said, "I hope that the Lord will give me enough strength from my casket to lift my right leg and kick that casket open and raise up and scream, "Lord, it ain't so. I had a lot of enemies." I think his point is well taken.

Why do you think the apostle was stoned in Lystra? He preached something that did some good. Why do you think that Bill Wallace had his head crushed against a cell in China— because he was preaching the forceful gospel both in life and in word, and in deed and in death. Why do you think that John the Baptist lost his head—because he preached the truth. Why do you think that John was exiled to the Isle of Patmos— because he was worth too much to the cause of good for those who supported evil to like him. So, they got rid of him. Why do you think Joan of Arc was burned at the stake—because she stood for something.

There's never been a prophet, there's never been a leader, there's never been a president, there's never been a states-man, there's never been any great man who stood for something whom everybody liked. When a man stands his ground, especially for God, there are some people who aren't going to like it. One of the worst things that will ever be said about a man is that, "Everybody loved him." All of us want to be popular. All of us do! We want to be liked. We want to be loved. But more than that, we must be loved of God for the truth of our lives. When the gospel of Jesus Christ comes, it causes contrasting reactions.

This Prescription Is the Only Cure We Have

Now when Paul preached to the people in Antioch, he didn't simply preach about Jesus. You'll never find Paul saying, "I have decided to know no one but Jesus Christ." You'll never find Paul saying he only appreciated Jesus. From Corinth, Paul wrote this to the Christians in Rome, "When I come unto you, I shall come in the fulness of the blessing of the gospel of Christ" (Rom. 15:29). Paul was emphasizing the truth that all of us should know, that Jesus alone is not enough. Now note carefully—one of the greatest dangers in the gospel of Jesus Christ and one of the greatest problems in the church is that we are only preaching about Jesus. I'm sure that statement got your attention. It is possible to appreciate Jesus without knowing the gospel, without knowing the truth of it. Jesus Christ did not come simply to draw men to admire him. The Bible says that "the Son of man is come to seek and to save that which was lost" (Luke 19:10). Now if Jesus came to be a seeker, he is just like many others. Socrates came seeking wisdom. Rockefeller came seeking money. Einstein came seeking knowledge. Jesus Christ came to seek *and* to *save* those which were lost.

Every day across my desk I get articles, sermons, and reviews by men who are preaching Jesus, but they are not preaching the gospel. Jesus was kind. He loved his fellowman. Therefore, these men believe we ought to all go and march in Washington.

I agree with them that we ought to help our fellowman, but they are stopping short. They are preaching Jesus, but they are not preaching the gospel. Jesus loved the little children. Therefore, they conclude, we ought to build a lot of places for the little children. "We ought to do that and forsake this gospel preaching," some say. That's Jesus, but it's not the gospel. If we aren't careful in our world, we are going to find people who appeal to us because they tell only how wonderful Jesus is while refusing to preach his gospel—his power to redeem men. Paul did not say, "For I determined not to know any thing among you, save Jesus Christ, and him crucified" (1 Cor. 2:2). That's the gospel. It's the only cure.

You can't get to heaven just by liking some of the things Jesus did. If the world could have been saved by the ethical Jesus, he would have never died. The difference in heaven and hell is not culture, it is Christ. There are some who worship Christ's influence on music, art, and literature. They think because they are cultured they are saved. They are just cultured lost people. The only answer for the cure of the world's disease is the gospel.

Jesus Christ lived, he died, and without his blood, men are lost. Without his resurrection, men are lost. That's the gospel. This is the only cure for our world—the gospel, the total gospel of the Lord Jesus Christ.

I have preached the funerals of murderers and some who have been the very personification of sainthood. I've stood over the caskets of men who had flown abroad, men who had investments in several countries, men who had a closet full of clothes. I've stood over men who didn't have a suit until they died. I've stood over men whose hands never picked up any tool of manual labor; yet I've stood over caskets of men whose hands were rough with the toils of daily responsibilities and backbreaking jobs. But do you know something peculiar? The rich man looks just as dead as the poor man. The rich man doesn't look any more alive. The man who is educated, the man who has bragged about his intellectualism doesn't look any more alive than the man who didn't have the same opportunities.

I'm saying that death is the equalizer. A person who does not have anything to carry beyond death has nothing. So while we spend time building better homes or putting clothes on people's backs which, by the way, is something Jesus would have us to do—if we do only that, we have let them die and go to hell as better educated or better dressed. That's all we've done. We have done nothing if we haven't told him about the gospel of Jesus Christ and that he died on the cross.

This Gospel Is Never Outdated

When Paul preached there were no automobiles traveling in front of that temple. There was no newspaper coming to his home every morning saying, "Rocket ships are putting capsules in orbit to circle our globe." There was nothing about heart transplants. There was nothing about electricity flashing through the dark night to lighten the skies that man might see. There were no stories about Polaris submarines that go under the water with a bomb fifteen times more explosive than the one dropped on Hiroshima. It was a simple day. Paul preached about a simple Jew who came as the Son of God and died on the cross.

When you and I look at our society, when we look at our affluence, it's hard to imagine taking that Jew from heaven and placing him down in our time and finding him compatible with our world. That's difficult, isn't it? What does an anti-quated Nazarene have to say to us? We are affluent, educated, cultured, rich, well-fed. What does he have to say to us?

Hear this! Men may go around this world in capsules powered by rocketships, but that can never take the place of the One who said, "I go to prepare a place for you" (John 14:2). Man might have every financial security known, but he needs to read the Scripture, "underneath are the everlasting arms"

(Deut. 33:27). Man might come to the time when everything can be done by the pushing of buttons and pulling of switches, but all of those buttons and all of those switches can never do what the drops of tears at Gethsemane did and the drops of blood at Calvary accomplished. It cannot do it. In our world we might get to the point where medical science can increase our age span far beyond one hundred years, but there is still the arresting message that says, "But after this the judgement" (Heb. 9:27).

Don't get confused in this modern rush and hurry-up world about that bronze Nazarene called Jesus Christ. Without him your life is nothing. In a real sense we don't have any more than people did in the first century. Man is lost without Jesus Christ. He can be saved and justified if he has been born again. He can go to heaven. He can reject Christ and spend eternity in hell.

You see, we are no different from those who rode camels, wrapped crude cloth around their bodies, and ate the few meager meals they were able to have. What's your problem, prescription or dosage? Do you know the truth and have you taken it? Do you believe in the gospel on the inside? I ask you to come to the gospel and live a life that causes others to make a judgment about you and to know how important Christ is.

7
Who Says So?

(Acts 13:4-12)

Not only is what is being said important but also who is saying it. Self-appointed authorities on every subject from horses to religion loudly, without encouragement, speak confidently about their subjects. The real problem with these persons is that they often convince some seeking inquirer that they ought to be heard.

Many of these deluded souls are in the world today. They are saying, "Come and follow us!" And because they speak with apparent authority, some people do follow after them. These self-appointed authorities may be sick, dirty, and worthless outcasts of society or well-dressed, college-educated people. No one asks, "Who says?" so they are listened to. They appear to be paragons of wisdom but are actually as shallow as mist on a sidewalk.

Our Lord never cared for these false prophets. In fact, he had more to say about them than he did the wrongness of the sinners' sin. He knew their hypocritical nature was a product of Satan himself.

The apostle Paul ran into one of these false prophets and pronounced an effective curse of blindness on him (Acts 13:4-12). Paul asked himself who this man was to speak in this manner. He wasn't about to be swayed by evil doctrine. This encounter has some valuable lessons.

The Loudest Voice May Not
Always Be the Wisest

When Paul arrived at Salamis with Mark, he discovered a man by the name of Elymas who had a strong following. We are not told what this man was preaching, but we are told enough to know that he was a representative of evil. He was better liked by others than Paul, who gave him one of the bitterest denunciations ever.

Paul knew that this man could seriously hamper the gospel because of his following. It was truly a case of the blind leading the blind. Paul knew, as we know, that a loud voice and a few naive constituents do not mean the cause is valid or worthwhile.

We are faced, today, with observing this same kind of phenomenon. Certain contemporary "knowns" are speaking loudly enough to gain some attention, but that for which they stand is undesirable. By some odd happenstance they are able to catapult themselves into the spotlight. They begin to speak—whether as wise men or idiots—and crowds began to gather.

What are we going to do with this type of person? What are we going to do when he speaks so loudly and people begin to follow his steps? One man has said, "I think it's wonderful to be immoral." Men buy his magazine by the millions. Even though this man is preoccupied with sex, millions of people are listening to his sensual garbage that is against that which we have known as good, honest, pure, and right. Some people have not yet learned, as Paul and John Mark learned, the loudest voice is not always the wisest voice. Young people need to learn it and adults need to learn it. We all need to come to grips with it.

Another loud but sad voice I am hearing all too frequently, "Well, Preacher, I believe in freedom of religion, but I'm not going to make my children go to church. I'm not going to force them." It's a strange thing to me though that they don't give their children a choice on which side of the highway to drive. They don't give them a choice whether they're going to start to school. They don't give them a choice about what kind of friends they want them to have. Yet the most important thing in the world is left up to chance and an immature mind.

I have never known any man who really quit church because parents lovingly taught him that the church was the first primary in his life. The bad experiences occur because the parents didn't go themselves, because parents and other adults were hypocrites, were spiritually low class, or were literally unrelated to the deep matters of the church. You may find a man who is not going to church today because his daddy forced him to go when he was a boy, but it will be about as rare as a boy who can't read and write because somebody forced him to attend school.

I read recently of a man who made a dynamo battery cell and was going to use it to provide a little light on his house, but after awhile the light flickered and went out and the battery cell would no longer produce a light. Finally, a science teacher friend of his said, "You can't use it to make a light any more, but I believe you have enough power to make a bell." So he made a bell. There are a lot of people in our world like this. They haven't got enough power to bring light to anybody, but they can make a lot of noise.

Wake up! Be alert! Listen to the apostle Paul when he ridiculed this man with a loud voice and a large following. Paul said, "Thou child of the devil" (Acts 13:10). That's the first lesson. The second one is this.

Silence Is Not Always a Virtue

Discovering Elymas preaching an evil doctrine, Paul was angered to an unbelievable extent. Paul looked at this man and, rather than talking about him, said directly to him, "Thou child of the devil." I wonder why Paul called him that? He said, "O full of all subtilty and all mischief . . . thou enemy of all righteousness." There are the reasons Paul got so angry.

First of all, the sorcerer was a Jew and so was Paul. I think that's one reason Paul might have gotten angry. He looked at this man and wanted to say, "Don't you know, friend, that you are a Jew? That you were raised in the shadow of God's tabernacle? You know the story of God's deliverance from Egypt. You have known how God has blessed us as he has blessed no other people. Here you are raised in the fellowship of the church; yet you are going outside of the will of God. You are blaspheming his name."

Here was a man brought up to respect God's way as a Jew; yet, when he got away from the confines of Judaism and the influence of godliness, he completely forgot all that he had been taught.

It's a sad thing when a child grows up, goes off to college, hears a professor try to shake his faith, and suddenly he is an intellect. Oh, if he were faced with some of the great spiritual giants of the day, he would have to lower himself and say, "I am nothing at all."

I recommend that you come back to the faith that your mothers and fathers taught you—that made them the mothers and fathers they are. You ought to thank them for the wisdom to rear you in a home of spiritual principles and say to them, "Thank God for the kind of Christian home that you have given me." It's high time all of us realized that silence is not always a virtue.

I think there is a second reason Paul should have been angered—this man had influence. I don't think Paul would have said all of these evil things about this man had he known that he had absolutely no following at all. Had he been a hermit, living in a cave, scratching himself with stones, and forgetting about everyone else around him, I think Paul would have said to Elymas, "Go your way, go your way, my friend. You'll be all right. Forget about it." But there was Sergius Paulus whom the Bible calls a prudent man. And he was shoulder to shoulder with this evil man; this sorcerer, this man Elymas. Sergius Paulus was being influenced by Elymas.

Many people think this is where Paul got his name, because he thought so much of his first convert that he named himself after this man. Others do not agree, believing that Paul got his name from the Latin word, Paulus, which means little. Paul said of himself, "I am the least of the apostles." In any event he looked at Elymas and said something like, "You devil, you son of a devil. You're trying to influence Sergius Paulus and drag him down."

There are those who are leading their weaker brothers down a primrose path of deception and evil. We must do something about it. No one ever goes to hell alone.

A third reason Paul's anger was justified was because of the name the man had chosen for himself. Do you know what the name *Bar* means in Hebrew? It means "son of." Do you realize what this man was calling himself? He was saying he was a son of Jesus, Bar-jesus. Paul was angered because this man called himself by Jesus' name in order to deceive others into believing that he was respectable and dependable. He wanted the people to think he was following the ways of the man who had died and was buried and was resurrected.

And do you know what angers good people today? People who claim to be Christians—Barchrist, sons of Christ—and yet live completely uncontrolled and unharnessed by the Spirit of God. Many people may be wondering whether Christians are really the sons of God or sons of the devil.

This kind of person was ridiculed by Paul. Paul spoke harsh words to him. I think we might have demon-possessed people in our city, demon-possessed people in our world, who are totally against pure righteousness—the holiness of Christ and the kingdom of God.

What does this have to do with what I am writing about—
Who Says So? We're not the only ones who ask this question.
When we begin to speak against the sins of the day, someone
is inevitably going to ask, "Who said that?" "Where did you
hear that?" "Who says so?" The answer comes back, "Well,
brother Christian says so." "Oh, he did—is that right? Why,
he has so much sin in his life, I don't see how he can afford
to say that." You see, the world asks too. People want to know
what authority I have and what authority you have. That's
why I have tried to take to heart the advice of a preacher
uncle of mine. He said, "Bailey, whatever else you do, however
good you preach, however excellent you are in organization,
keep your life above reproach." How can a man speak about
one sin when there is a blacker sin in his own life? How can
a deacon stand against one sin when there is a deeper sin
in his own life? How can a Sunday School teacher stand against
one sin when he has a more serious sin in his own life? The
world will always ask, "Who says so?"

The world is asking, "Who says so?" What if someone had
stood up to Jesus when he chased those money-changers out
of the Temple and asked, "Who are you?" No one did, however. No one grabbed his arm. No one tried to tackle or man-
handle him. Why? Because they knew his life was above reproach. They knew he was close to God. If they had caught
Jesus cheating somebody or desecrating the Temple before
that, they wouldn't have had any respect for Jesus at all. They
probably would have ganged up on him and said, "We don't
have to listen to you, you hypocrite." His holiness was so evident, the people knew his actions were consistent with his
living.

The world, young people and adults alike, is looking for
somebody who has a deep faith that will not waiver no matter
what, a faith that will not give in. The world needs people
who will not waiver just because some associates say, "Give
in," because some groups say, "Give in," because some impor-

tant persons in their lives say, "Give in." What the world needs to see is a man who will speak out against the evils of the world, for he, like Paul, is filled with the Holy Spirit. We don't hear much speaking against sin any more because most of us have so much in our lives that we can't find anything outside of our lives to talk about.

Silence is not always a virtue. There are times when you need to speak as Paul spoke. But remember, the only time you and I can afford to speak is when we've been on our knees in prayer. We must be examples.

A man got on a bus and was given too much change by the bus driver. He came back to the bus driver and said, "Sir, you gave me too much change—I'd like to give the money back."

The bus driver said, "Thank you, Preacher."

The man was astonished. "How did you know I was a preacher?"

"Well, I was in your church last night and I heard you preach on stealing and I intentionally gave you too much change to see if you were honest enough to bring it back. I just wanted to know if you practiced what you preached."

You see, there are people all over the world who are asking about me and about deacons and Sunday School teachers and about all laymen: "Who says so?" "What right do they have?" "How clean of a vessel are they to harbor the Spirit of God in their life?"

I challenge each of us to make our lives so pure, so upright and clean, so dedicated to God that we can speak out against the evils of our day and get a sympathetic hearing. You see, the world is asking, "Do you have a right to speak out?" We do if we, as Paul, are filled with the Spirit of God. When someone asks, "Who says so?" and someone else gives our names, they might very well reply, "Well, he certainly lives a good life. Maybe I ought to try it. He certainly lives what he believes."

8
You Don't Have to Go On!

(Acts 13:13)

With my imagination I can see young John Mark with his hands clasped together, his arms pulling his folded knees up toward his chest. He is gazing up at the star-speckled sky. The campfire nearby sends a breath of smoke to his eyes, blurring his vision for a moment. His two companions, Paul and Uncle Barnabas, lay sleeping just beyond the glittering fire. John Mark wishes for that kind of sleep, but it eludes him in spite of all he can do.

Some time before, Mark had pleaded to go with these two older men on what he thought would be an exciting and romantic adventure. He had no idea it would be like this. Why this very day, they had faced death, hunger, anger of mobs, and worst of all for young Mark, loneliness. He is seriously disillusioned with the whole affair.

He cannot hold his thoughts back any longer. He jumps up and wakes Paul and says, "Paul, I've got blisters on my feet that I could walk on if I had no feet at all. I've got callouses on my hands, and my body is dirty. Paul, we need to go back. There is work to do in Jerusalem; there are responsibilities there, people to win, Jews to convert, and Gentiles to win. Paul, let's go back."

Paul says to the young John Mark, his helper, "John, I'm sorry I can't go back. I've put my hand to the plow and there's no turning back for me."

Finally in frustration, the young man looks over at his uncle and bends down on the dirt beside the blanket spread upon the ground and says, "Uncle Barnabas, could you reason with Paul? Could you tell him that we have gone all day? If we have traveled one mile, we have traveled fifty miles and I just can't take it any longer. I bet we haven't had five converts today. We could have been doing more good back at Jerusalem."

Barnabas looks at Paul and asks him what he thinks, and Paul resolutely shakes his head and says, "No, I can't go back."

Barnabas says to his young nephew, "But Mark, you understand that I've got to stay too because I'm going with Paul."

"This is a useless affair. You men are crazy. You've lost your minds. My body is aching with pain. We are going to meet every kind of difficulty in the world. You men are out of your minds to try to build a church in this way," Mark says.

Finally Paul can't stand it any longer; he jumps to his feet, looks at John Mark, and says, "John Mark, Barnabas and I are going to stay, but you can go on. Go on back, John Mark. Go on back to your soft bed, to plenty of water, to food, and to the comfort of the house; go on if you want to. You don't have to go on with us. You don't have to go on."

This brings us to our passage Scripture in the book of Acts. Paul has taken a young man with them by the name of John Mark, the nephew of Barnabas. Barnabas is a good man, a noble man; a man the Bible says was fair with his finances, a man whom everybody loved.

In Acts 13:13 we read, "Now when Paul and his company loosed from Paphos, they came to Perga in Pamphylia: and John departing from them returned to Jerusalem." It's amazing how Luke, the writer of Acts, doesn't say anymore. He doesn't give any explanation; he does not offer any excuses; he doesn't try to use any rational reasoning why John Mark would do this, but for some reason or another John Mark departed.

As I began this chapter I imagined that this probably was the routine that happened. John Mark certainly did not want to go back alone. It would have been greater comfort for him if he could have convinced Paul and Barnabas that this was a useless journey, that the sacrifices made were too great, and that the demands were too far-reaching. If they went back with him, no one would think anything about his coming home, giving up the task, and forsaking his responsibilities. But Paul and Barnabas wouldn't listen. They decided to go on.

John Mark returned home. And this is what I want to write about now. *You don't have to go on.* Look at the passage of Scripture if you will and think of the story. *You don't have to go on because:*

The Work Will Be Done Without You Anyway

As Paul and Barnabas left for Antioch of Pisidia, they were just as tired as Mark and maybe more tired because they were older men. But they had more courage for some reason. They had not recently been pampered by a loving mother. Whatever made John Mark go back, it is of little concern to us, but he did go back. Paul and Barnabas went on, not stopping because one man did not have the courage to go on. They went on about their job.

I think there might have been a time when Paul needed something to be done and turned around to say, "John Mark, if you would please go get the . . . ." Paul probably thought to himself, How silly am I, how unthoughtful of me, John Mark left us two days ago; he is not here to help us anymore. And it could have been that Barnabas, at a time of need, might have said to his young nephew, "John Mark, if you would, please come with me over to this city." Then Barnabas began to remember that Mark had left them. They had depended on him, and they're missing him now; their work is more difficult without him and the responsibilities are more concentrated upon fewer men because one man has left.

Thanks be to God for the way he works his work. The work keeps on. God's Word is still preached; the song leading is still done; offerings are still taken; souls are still won; churches are still established; people are still brought closer to God. The fact seems to ring from the Old Testament to the New Testament to the present—there is no one man upon which the kingdom of God rests.

Let the greatest pastor in all of the world resign his church, the church may well flourish and possibly be even better under another man. Let a great evangelist meet a tragic death, and God will reach down into some mother's womb and pull from her some evangelist who can speak in more eloquent terms and persuade thousands to come to the altar to repent of their sins and give their hearts to Jesus Christ. Let a great missionary be the target for the enemies' arrows. The world will weep over his death, but it isn't long until, in the mercy and providence of God, somebody born in the United States or on foreign soil will hear the voice of God on his Damascus Road. He will turn to God and will say, "Lord, here am I." It happens over and over again, for there just isn't any man in the world upon which rests the entire success or failure of the kingdom of God.

Moses probably thought he was important at a time, but God said something like, "Moses, you are not that important and because you disobeyed me at a time, you are not going to get to come into the Promised Land."

Well, when those Hebrews (they didn't know it at the time Moses did) were going into Canaan and learned that the great leader, Moses, was not going to go—they were downhearted; they were so distressed; they were so beside themselves they could not believe it. They said to themselves, "God has brought us from the flesh pots of Egypt to let the buzzards pick our bones clean of our flesh and die upon the very border line of the Promised Land. He has prohibited Moses from being our leader. He has let Moses go upon the mountain and die."

But God said, "Wait a moment, there's another man. The world does not depend upon Moses." A young handsome man by the name of Joshua became the leader and led the people into the Promised Land. For every time a Moses has disobeyed God and must die and leave his job unfulfilled, there shall be a Joshua to come and take his place and to lead God's people where they ought to go.

I shall never forget a funeral service I attended one time. I think the minister meant well when he said, "Brother So and So has been working for the Lord off and on for the last forty years." I think this could be well said of many people, of many Baptists—"They've worked on and off for the Lord, but many of them mostly off." Here for the Lord, there for the devil, but a lot of times "off for the Lord." The kingdom of God does not rest upon one man.

You see, just because some people are lazy and quit their jobs, God isn't going to give up his business. You don't have to go on if you don't want to! But God's work will continue. You don't have to teach next year. You don't have to work in Bible School. You don't have to perform your responsibilities. You don't have to go on, but God's work will. God's work will find somebody who is a Joshua, who is willing to say yes to the responsibilities.

God looked one time at a man by the name of Abel and said, "Abel, what do you have in your hand?"

Abel said, "Nothing but a lamb, Lord."

God said, "Put it on the altar." Abel took the lamb and put it on the altar and the smoke from that altar has been bringing a savory smell into the nostrils of multitudes throughout the years.

God looked at a man by the name of Moses, and said, "Moses, what do you have in your hand?"

Moses said, "Nothing, God, but a rod."

God said, "Moses, lift that rod over the sea and that sea shall depart and the children of Israel shall walk across on dry land and Pharaoh's armies will be drowned." Moses used what he had for God, and it became something great.

There was a woman in the Bible by the name of Dorcas, and God looked down upon her and said, "Dorcas, what do you have in your hand?"

Dorcas said, "I don't have anything but a needle and thread, God."

God said, "Dorcas, use it," and the garment she made has been the pattern for Christian womanhood down through the ages. She knew that when a person lets God use what she has, God can do something with it. Dorcas used what she had and Abel used what he had and Moses used what he had.

John Mark, you don't have to go on—the work will go on without you. You don't have to go on.

You'll Miss a Great Adventure if You Don't Go

You don't have to go on, but you'll miss life's greatest adventure. Who do you think lost the most in the story of John Mark? John Mark came to Paul and Barnabas and said, "I just can't go on."

Paul said, "You don't have to go on. Go on back to Jerusalem; go on back and let your mother take care of you. Go back to her apronstrings. Go on where it's easy." John Mark went on back. I can imagine as Mark got into his soft clothes and into that soft bed, he thought to himself, Oh, I wonder what is going on in Antioch. I'm not very tired, my feet don't hurt and my muscles don't ache. Oh, it would be great to be with Paul and Barnabas!

Did you know that one of the results of idleness is the continuance of a lack of duty? John Mark tried to do some things, the Bible tells us, but he failed in all that he did because when he refused to do the thing that God wanted him to do. He discovered that the things he tried to do on his own merit, outside the will of God, were absolutely useless. John Mark was the loser. John Mark missed those times when Paul preached and Barnabas spoke and gave his testimony. He missed seeing people say yes to God.

John Mark even missed the shipwrecks. You say, "missed them?" Yes, for you see those people who have done the most for the kingdom of God, and those people who love Jesus most, and those people who have more concern about the church are those people who have a pocketbook a little thinner, a heart a bit richer, a soul a little bit fuller, and a life a little bit more worn because they have done something for the kingdom of God. The losing person in the church of God is the one who stands back and watches the forward thrust of the church, go on and on and on. My friend, the greatest trip in all of the world is to go forward into the thick of the battle in a local church for the sake of Jesus Christ. Nothing can you do better in your life. That's where the water hits the wheel.

I'll never forget when I was pastor near Lake Village, Arkansas. Occasionally I visited a family whose name I have fortunately forgotten. They worked, they ate, and they took their boat on Sunday and went water skiing or fishing. They lived that kind of life. They ate to work and worked to eat. Fleshly pleasure was the keynote of their life. Do you know what they used to laugh about? (This is not to make fun of people in this condition because some can't help it.) The lady used to sit in a big chair and just giggle and giggle and shake like Mrs. Santa Claus and say, "You know, we're kind of known around here as the Fat Family, Ha, Ha, Ha." And they were, all of them. They not only had fat bodies but also they had fat hearts, fat souls, and fat consciences. I couldn't imagine how a person could go through life like that; there are a lot of skinny ones like that, by the way. The only purpose they have in life is for self. They want to feed self, recreate self, please self, entertain self, and watch self grow fat without a real burden for the cause of Christ.

You don't have to go on for the church; you don't have to go on with its great programs; you don't have to go on when the times are rough and the sacrifices are demanded. You can go rest in your Jerusalem easy chair if you want to and let some of the rest of us sweat and bleed; you can come back when the battle is over and claim the victory. But my friend, the greatest privilege in a church is to give up something to be close to Jesus Christ. John Mark didn't know that. He wanted to go back. He wasn't willing to take a risk.

What if Jesus Christ had not been willing to risk something? Do you know what he would have done? He would have taught in the Temple. He would have been good to the little children. He would have been a great example to the world; but when it came time for the cross, Jesus Christ would have said, "I can't do it, I can't risk that."

But God would have looked down at Jesus and said, "Jesus, you don't realize that if you'll do this, this will help the world to be redeemed."

Jesus could have looked back to glory and said, "God, I'm not that kind of a gambler. I can't gamble my life that men will come back to you, to righteous living. I can't do that; I can't risk that." But Jesus didn't do that. He obeyed God and let God take care of the other. He went to the cross and died that men might be redeemed.

Gypsy Smith was once asked by a lady to come to speak to a small group. The lady said, "Brother Smith, you won't have to worry about anything, it's just a small group—it won't take much out of you."

Gypsy Smith looked at the lady and he said, "Lady, I don't preach any place that it doesn't take a lot out of me." Life's greatest adventure is when you give and you give until Jerusalem is a bitter sound in your ears and Antioch of Pisidia and its wood and its beasts and its hatred become a joy and a challenge to your life.

If You Don't Go, God Hopes You'll Come Back

John Mark decided not to go on and how disappointed his friends were. Later on the book of Acts records a bitter disagreement between Paul and Barnabas over whether John Mark should go with them again. Do you know what happened? John Mark became concerned and repentant. John Mark began to consider what he had done to Paul and Barnabas, and he was sorry his lack of commitment caused an extra burden on them.

It would be good if church members would realize that when they say no, their share of the load shifts to other people. It makes others have to do more. You see, everybody could have a reason to say no, but some say, "I'll do it in spite of my needs—in spite of my responsibilities."

John Mark quit. He went back. He was satisfied for a while, but the work of the kingdom of God came on him in such a pressure that he came back. He came back and became another missionary for the sake of Christ. He wrote one of the most beautiful Gospels in the Bible—Mark. It is one of the most detailed books that we have of the life of our Lord. John Mark saw that, even though he forsook the work, there was a responsibility for him to come back.

You might be able to describe an incident in your life that's much like John Mark's. You saw the responsibilities and duties ahead but you just said to yourself, "I cannot go on." You didn't have to go on. The kingdom of God can go on without you but you'll miss life's greatest adventure.

You can come back, however. There is always a book to be written; there's always a job to be done; there's always a mission field to be crossed; there's always a debt to be paid; there's always a testimony to be given; there's always a floor to be swept; there's always a considerate word to be given to the bereaved; there's always something to do if you'll come back. Some of you are sitting in your reclining chairs of Jerusalem. Some of you are watching while the Pauls and Barnabases of this world do the work and make the sacrifices and you take the glory. You don't have to stay there. John Mark didn't. He went back, became a missionary, and wrote a book. When Paul was close to his death, he said, "Bring [Mark] with thee: for he is profitable to me for the ministry" (2 Tim. 4:11).

You are away, you are outside of God's will, but you don't have to be. You can come back. Failure does not have to be final. If you're willing as John Mark was, to be sorry for your neglect, just pray, "God help me to be a Mark who comes back to the responsibilities of work and to sacrifice." Anyone can sit in Jerusalem, but it takes somebody dedicated to fight the battle. You don't have to go on, but the glory of the presence of God you get along the way is worth the effort of the journey. Keep on going. You'll be eternally glad you did.

9
Renewal or Reaffirmation?

(Acts 13:14-52)

There is much talk today about renewal in the church. A conglomeration of modern thinkers are saying, "Let's do away with the old cloak of the church and slip into a more comfortable garment." The church needs "a new image," as one man has stated. Scores of other voices, desiring to be heard, admit that they feel the church needs—because it is wrinkled a place or two—a professional face-lifting. So they say the church must have renewal.

I agree that the church is due for a thorough change. I would have to vote with those who say something is wrong. But I couldn't disagree with them more on what the church needs.

The church is not so much in need of renewal as it is in need of reaffirmation. In fact, it is the continual renewing that has gotten the church off-center. We have a new timidity about sin when we need to reaffirm again "that the wages of sin is death." We have the new permissiveness, but need to reaffirm, "Present your bodies a living sacrifice" (Rom. 12:1), and "your body is the temple of the Holy Ghost" (1 Cor. 6:19).

The church of Jesus Christ will never go forward until first it goes backward. The truth is well illustrated in Billy Graham's statement when a British columnist said of his London Crusade, "Billy Graham has set Christianity in England back two hundred years." Graham later retorted, "I was trying to set it back two thousand years."

Acts 13:14-52 records Paul's first sermon. Paul chose to preach the gospel to Jews in this Gentile city of Antioch in Pisidia. He probably could have impressed them with his great and wide-ranging knowledge, but he did not. He said some things to those men that I feel certain should be reaffirmed in our day. If we are ever going to hope for results like Peter's and Paul's, we are going to have to preach the message of Peter and Paul.

Why should we reaffirm these truths of God's Word? There are two important reasons. The truths of the gospel are too important to neglect. Secondly, the gospel is the only thing God promises to bless. Paul preached to the basic doctrines of the gospel.

The Sovereignty of God

Look at what Paul preached. He preached to the Jewish people the sovereignty of God. Now if there is anything we need to reaffirm in our day, it is the sovereignty of God. Paul said "The God of this people of Israel chose our fathers" (v. 17). Notice verse 19, "And when he had destroyed seven nations in the land of Chanaan, he divided their land to them by lot." God was on somebody's side, the side of those he had chosen and picked out. Notice, if you will, verse 48, "And when the Gentiles heard this, they were glad, and glorified the word of the Lord: and as many as were ordained to eternal life believed."

In his first sermon, Paul knew that one of the greatest facts of all Christianity was (as it was a great fact of the Old Testament) that God is a sovereign God. He does not have to fall into the logic of man. He does not have to do what man counts fair. He does not have to abide by the rules of what man says is reasonable. When you talk about the sovereignty of God, you are admitting that God has a right to do anything that he wants to.

Since the day of Adam, man had been depraved. Man chose

against God. Man chose sin. God chose a group of people by the name of Israel and chose them to be his people; to spread his truth around this world. And the amazing thing about it is that while scores of people today can believe that God chose Israel and allowed Israel to defeat this group and that group and another group, that same person has problems in believing that today. God in his own sovereign will, in his own elective processes, reaches down into America, in Europe, or in any other continent, and places his hand upon a person and that person is born again.

Now you don't come to the converse. There's nothing in the Bible about God choosing people to be lost. There's nothing here about God electing people to go to hell. But there is a great deal of doctrine about God being the one who chooses people to be saved. Difficult to understand? God, in his elective purpose, reached down and picked me and you out as his chosen people. Do you believe he chose Israel? If you do, you can believe he chooses us.

A theologian stood before a large gathering of people and said, "Nobody can be saved just anytime he wants to." When I first heard the statement, I almost wondered if this man was guilty of infidelity to the truth of God. Then he repeated, "No man can come to be saved just any old time he wants to be saved." And he's right. The Bible itself says, "No man can come to me, except the Father which hath sent me draws him." Every person who has ever been saved upon the face of the earth experiences the initiating act of God.

We don't have any power to be saved. We don't have the wisdom and the knowledge to know how to respond to God. But in his elective grace, he places his hands upon boys and girls, men and women, and his Spirit convicts of sin. We are chosen of him to be a part of his great kingdom. He doesn't choose anybody to be lost. There's no doctrine about that. There *is* a doctrine about God's elective power and purpose in almost every letter that Paul wrote.

Whosoever will may come? Yes! But those who come are those whom God has placed his hand upon to come. Why did Paul teach it? Why is it in the Scripture? It is there because of the responsibility it puts on me and you. Think about it. Do you know that God chose you to be saved? Do you know that God chose you Sunday School teacher and director? Do you know, preacher, that God chose you? Paul indicated in a later letter, "He hath chosen us in him before the foundations of the world." Before I was born, God knew that one day Bailey Smith would be born to Bailey Ezell Smith and to Frances Amber Lucky Smith. God also knew that when I was ten years old I would be born again by the elective grace and power of God.

What does that do to you? I'll tell you what it ought to do. It ought to make you look into your heart and say, "If God chose me before the foundation of the earth, what a responsibility it places on me and my life." It ought to challenge all of us. It ought to move us to great things to know that God thinks of us individually.

Don't worry about who gets elected. You go and you witness and teach others; you help and plead for them to be God's people. Even the desire to be saved is the initiating, elective power of God. He does it. What a responsibility it puts upon you and upon me. Now that doctrine is too precious not to reaffirm. Paul was affirming God's sovereignty. God can do what he wants to, whether we like it or understand it. God is sovereign.

Man Is a Sinner

Paul then preached to them that man is a sinner. Paul told them about Jesus Christ scourged in Pilate's hall. He told them that the reason Jesus Christ was scourged and the reason he died on the cross was because of the sins of the Jews and Gentiles alike who let him die there.

If we aren't careful, the cross of Jesus Christ will begin to mean for you and me only a place where a criminal was placed because he got caught in going against the rules of the government. Paul said that Jesus died on the cross for the remission of sins. Do you know that Jesus Christ died on the cross because we are worthless, sin-filled, and rotten without a hope in the world? The reason we need to reaffirm the truth of the gospel is for man to know that he is a sinner. He is lost. The cross is a result of sin. It's not the result of a criminal being caught. Blood was shed that I might be saved. You are a sinner. I am a sinner. Our hearts are black. Our sin nature will land us in hell. That's too important to neglect.

Some say, "Oh, I don't believe Jesus Christ or God would send anybody to hell." When a person says that, they are saying, "I don't believe God would send anybody as nice and wholesome as I am to hell." I wonder why they don't turn that around. Ask the question, How can a holy, righteous, omnipotent God come and die to save one man, much less the whole world? How can a holy God become sin? We shouldn't be asking how can God send somebody to hell. We ought to be asking how God can save anybody as selfish and sinful as we are.

Christ's Rejectors Spend Eternity in Hell

Paul said, "But seeing you put it from you, and judge yourselves unworthy of everlasting life, lo, we must turn to the Gentiles" (Acts 14:46). Do you know what Paul was saying here? "You're going to hell if that's what you want to do. Some of you judge yourselves to everlasting death, lo, we turn our backs upon you, we go to preach to somebody who will hear us; we shake the dust of responsibility from our shoes; we go to somebody else. If you want to go to hell, that's your business." That's a doctrine too important to neglect. That's why I say not renewal, but reaffirmation is needed in our churches. Do you know there are some people today who are still having difficulty with that kind of a truth?

A shallow-thinking man said, "I wouldn't give a snap of my finger to save a man from hell or to help a man go to heaven, but I will give my life to make a little bit less hell on earth and a little more heaven where man lives." A man is not much of a preacher, not much of a pastor, who just wants to make earth heaven. I agree that we need to do something about the world's condition. We ought to do something about water pollution. We ought to do something about unfairness. We ought to do something about social injustices. We ought to do something about all of the diseases of our land. We ought to do something about discrimination. While we are doing something about that, we must not forget the reaffirmation of the truths of Jesus Christ that have built the church from the earliest days—and one is the truth of hell.

Look at this phrase, *hell on earth*. A lot of people will say war is hell. But you know that is not so because in war the Red Cross occasionally comes along. Listen lost friend; there's not going to be any Red Cross to help you in hell. There's not going to be any place where you can go to a hospital and find a little care. Hell on earth? Don't kid yourself. There's not going to be any place where you can have an occasional drink of water. There's not going to be any music. There's not going to be any laughter. There are not going to be any words of comfort. There's not going to be any kind hand on your brow. There's no such thing as hell on earth. Earth can never come close to being what hell really is.

Revelation says, "Whosoever was not found written in the book of life was cast into the lake of fire (Rev. 20:15). Where's that on earth? The psalmist said, "The wicked shall be turned into hell" (Ps. 9:17). Where on earth is that? Jesus, who talked about Gehinna (the garbage dump near Jerusalem) said, hell is a place "where their worm dieth not, and the fire is not quenched." Do you have that around your place? Is that any place on earth? There are no difficulties, heartaches, tragedies, or sacrifices that can approximate what is in store for the person who says no to Jesus Christ. It is hell—eternal fire. It is damnation. It is torment. It is eternal separation from God. This is why we don't need renewal—we need reaffirmation. Look at some of our cold, dead churches where people come to hear all of the pretty, perfumed sermons. If men would tell the people out in the congregation that unless Jesus is their Savior they are going to hell, we might have some old-fashioned religion that would do something for people instead of letting them be satisfied in their sins and sure enough going to hell. The only way we are going to get people out of hell is to get more of preaching about hell in the pulpit. Reaffirmation is our need—not something new, not something revolutionary that has come from the twentieth century, but something bold from God's Word.

Paul said God is sovereign. He said men are lost. He said those who reject Christ are lost without hope in the world.

An atheist heard a preacher preach the gospel and asked to debate him. The preacher said, "All right, I'll debate with you, Mr. Atheist, if you will bring with you ten people whose hearts have been made aglow, whose lives have been wonderfully made new because of your belief. I'll meet you at two o'clock at the auditorium. You bring with you ten people who have been marvelously transformed by atheism. I'm going to bring a hundred with me who have been marvelously transformed by the gospel of Jesus Christ. All you have to do is bring ten." The Christian preacher showed up and more than a hundred were behind him to speak out for the truth of the gospel. The atheist never showed up.

God chose you to be saved. Do you know that you are lost without hope and do you realize that the gospel of Jesus Christ can save you from eternal hell? Are you lost? What if you were to die this moment? Where would you spend eternity? Paul had an answer. The Bible has an answer. Jesus has an answer. Real Christianity is bound up in these truths. Believe them—love them—share them.

10

In Defense of Disturbing

(Acts 14:1-7)

Does the church have a right to disturb us? Or, is it more the duty of the church to "leave us be," no matter in what condition it finds us? Is the church nothing but a large doting grandparent that holds our hands on just any path we choose to walk? Or, does the church have, inherent in its own purpose, a divine obligation to pull us to other paths with more beneficial designations and safer routes—even if that pull might occasionally be a sharp jerk.

A sharp jerk? Why would that ever be necessary? Because paths have a way of becoming ruts when traveled so often, and it's never easy to get out of a rut. Of course, the church could leave us there with less effort on her part and very little disturbance on ours. Should she? I think not.

After the tragic explosion in the Texas City School some years ago that took over three hundred young lives, an investigator heard a lady say, "Why, my husband knew that gas leak was there, but he didn't say anything about it."

The stunned inquirer said, "Your husband knew?"

"Yes, he did," said she.

"Well, lady," said the inquirer, "you are married to a criminal."

Is this not the position of the church—to warn us of the error of our ways? Is it not wiser for the church to disturb us for awhile than to allow us to destroy ourselves for an eternity?

In our Scripture for this chapter (Acts 14:1-7), we find a group of unbelieving Jews trying to stir up some seeking Gentiles. If the unbelievers are concerned about stirring up people to their way, how much more should the church, with an answer for every dilemma of man, be concerned?

In defense of the church's right and, more importantly, it's responsibility to disturb, I want us to consider the following.

This Is a Day When Disturbing Is Prevalent

Verse 2 says, "But the unbelieving Jews stirred up the Gentiles." What group of people were doing the stirring up? It was those people who had pushed Paul and Barnabas out. It was those who wanted to get a mob to run the missionaries out of town. The unbelieving Jews stirred up the Gentiles against Paul and Barnabas and said to them, "We don't want anything to do with you," and they began a whispering campaign. "You don't want anything to do with these men, for they are immoral, indecent, and they are fooling you about this Jesus Christ. They are making idiots out of you. They'll call you gullible and naive because they're going to exploit every sensitive nerve that you have. Get rid of them." So they started a whispering campaign.

Notice which group was getting the people stirred up. They were the unbelieving, those who were lost, those who were sinners, those who were anti-Christian, those who were against the great Paul and Barnabas. They were opposed to every good work that the church was doing. They stirred up the people.

Now why did they stir up the people? Because Paul and Barnabas had already stirred them up. They were trying to unstir them, if you can unstir anything. They wanted to undo what Paul and Barnabas had done. And when Paul and Barnabas began to stir up the people in such effectiveness, those who were anti-Christ began to tell lies and falsehoods about the men of God.

Now, I'm often disturbed when people begin to say, "The church doesn't have a right to upset us." "The church doesn't have a right to disturb us." But notice in this passage that the ones the Bible records doing the stirring were the unbelievers. "And the unbelieving Jews stirred up the Gentiles." If the unbelievers can be disturbing, there ought to be something in the world today which the church is disturbed about.

We are living in a world of disturbance. The word *disturbance* is not new. I think the church ought to be disturbed, as well as individuals, don't you? Evil is rampant all over our world. I think the church ought to be disturbed that *purity* is a word reserved for the age of buggies and high-top shoes. I think the church ought to be disturbed about some of the things that are permitted within our own country. I think the church ought to be disturbed because we have elected men who don't mind using the name of God in vain when they speak in public. I think the church ought to be disturbed when a college girl in California strips her body nude to win a campus election.

If the church is not disturbing people, then somebody else is. If the cause of good is not rousing people to fight, then something evil is. If moral living and righteous causes are not getting people to live the way God wants them to live, then dirt and filth are getting them disturbed for the devil. What's going to be our choice? *Disturbance* is a word that you and I are familiar with. We are disturbed about Iran. We are disturbed about the Cambodia situation. We are disturbed about Israel and Egypt. We are disturbed about Latin American problems. We have been disturbed for years about Berlin. Every now and then we become more disturbed about Korea. We are disturbed about internal conflicts. We are a disturbed nation.

If the Church of Jesus Christ Ever Fails to
Disturb Men, It Has Failed Completely

If the church of Jesus Christ ever fails to disturb, it has failed completely. Discover in verse 3 how Paul and Barnabas preached, "Long time therefore abode they speaking boldly in the Lord." "Long time." Do you know what that Greek word means? It means both types of length. It means for a long period of days and for a long period of time at each speaking time. They not only spoke for many days but also on the days they spoke, they spoke for a long time. They didn't have anybody watching the clock. They didn't have anybody worrying about the burned roast. They preached for a long time. That's amazing, isn't it? Nobody ever sues dance halls because they go overtime. Nobody ever gossips about them. None of the ladies quit the bridge club when they go a little bit past the time that's been designated. But let something spiritual, let something wholesome, go five minutes overtime, and some people get upset.

Again notice how Paul and Barnabas preached. They preached *boldly*. They preached with courage. You couldn't have walked out of that house after hearing those people preach and feel real good on the inside. You would have been disturbed. You would have been upset. You would have known something was wrong in your life. You would have known, once and for all, you were going to do something about it before it was too late.

Now note verse 1, "And it came to pass in Iconium that they went both together into the synagogue of the Jews, and so spake, that a great multitude . . . believed." "And so spake": what does the term "so spake" mean? It doesn't mean that Paul spoke with eloquence because when he wrote to that church in Corinth, he talked about his fear and trembling and his stuttering speech. Paul was not a great speaker. Paul was not a man who knew all the rules of rhetoric. But he and Barnabas "so spake" that multitudes of people came to God. They spoke with power and conviction.

Now it doesn't say that they "so spake" that people were calm and all of the city was at ease. It doesn't say that they "so spake" that people began to feel peace of mind because they had more confidence in themselves and everybody suddenly began to think positively. They "so spake" that a multitude of people came that day and were converted. They spoke believing with all of their hearts that the only hope is Jesus Christ and if a man doesn't have Jesus Christ, he is lost. He is bound for a devil's hell. He doesn't have a hope in the world. They "so spake" that people would believe.

Oh, that preachers would speak today that people would believe instead of yawning until they get through. Oh, that prophets would preach so people would be so convicted they couldn't walk out the front door before they were made right with God. Oh, that preachers would so speak today that Christians would come and bow their knees before Jehovah and say, "Lord, be merciful unto me a wayward and backslidden child of God and return unto me the joy of salvation."

So speak! So speak! In some churches if the pastor said anything that's outstanding, the congregation would be shocked. They don't expect it. Paul and Barnabas *so spake* that multitudes of people came unto them to find peace through Jesus Christ.

Notice this word in verse 4, "But the multitude of the city was divided." Here come two tentmakers into a calm city, and they begin to preach something those people didn't like (at least some of them didn't like it). Some people said to themselves, "Now, we've got to get rid of these tentmakers for they have upset our unanimity. We were a town of unanimity. We were bound together. We were peaceful. We had a lovely existence. We were as calm as we could be."

Sometimes peace is only a different name for death, and that's what it was in that city. I hope that my family will never have to live in a city that is all peaceful. You see, the Bible says as long as there are men and women on the face of the earth not all people will be for Jesus. So, if I find a place where everyone agrees with each other, that place is uncontrolled in any way by the will of God. I will fail to find any people who claim to use God's Word as their final authority. That's peace at too great a price. I guess a Communist state comes close to that.

Do you know one of the greatest tragedies in the world today is that a person cannot live in a city very long and really come to the conclusion that the city is divided? Why is that? Because a few Christians melt and mingle over into the wrong groups. A little bit of this group melts and mingles over into the Christians, and we fade in over here. We melt and mingle one with another until we become cities of dangerous unanimity. We don't need more peaceful cities. We don't need more unanimity. We don't need everybody in complete agreement if it means giving up strong principles of living a holy and righteous life. The world ought to see where the Christians stop and the non-Christians begin. There ought to be a difference. Our city ought to be divided. There ought to be a line that nobody can overlook. Now, if everyone had peace in Christ and unity in him, unanimity would be welcomed. Then, of course, that would also be heaven.

Iconium was divided because somebody upset the people. Somebody disturbed them and they began to look at themselves. Jesus said, "Think not that I am come to send peace on earth: I came not to send peace, but a sword. For I am come to set a man at variance against his father, and the daughter against her mother, and the daughter in law against her mother in law" (Matt. 10:34-35).

Now, those first Christians could have gotten by without disturbing people. The authorities might have approached the Christians and said, "Now we want you to have your God, but we want our god. You give us the same right. Your God can be one of those in the Parthenon. He can be as good as the rest of them." The Christians said no. They refused. They said that Jesus Christ was not one among gods. He had first place and every place or no place. They wanted to let everybody else know that there was only one God and that was Jesus. "Oh, Christians, be logical about it. Don't disturb our society. We've got our gods, you've got your gods." To such a statement those Christians would have said, "We would rather be fed to the lions than to say your god is as good as our God." And they were. They were not afraid to disturb anybody.

I believe with all of the sincerity of my heart that if we would begin to disturb a few folks, asking them if they've had an experience with Jesus Christ, asking them if they've been born again, we might have divided cities where people of God could really stand out for Jesus. Do you live in a divided city? Or, do you live in a mediocre city for the cause of absolutely nothing—one where Christians have blended perfectly into the decadence of their society?

In one of his sermons, Joseph Parker, a preacher of another generation, said he could imagine going into a great orchestra where hundreds of violins were being played. He would take one of those priceless instruments of Cremona and begin to play it with a true hand of a Paganini. He would hit all of the true tones and all of the beautiful music would come flowing from that beautiful instrument that he was playing—absolutely perfect, not one blemish, not one mistake. Those who were playing with mediocrity would begin to think to themselves, "We don't like this man. We don't like him because he's playing too well. He makes us look bad." Instead of everybody jumping and shouting and praising a man who was playing so beautifully, they would begin to hate him and to despise him.

Until your life begins to disturb some people, it may not be what it ought to be. Have you disturbed anybody lately because you are such a good Christian? You see, if you live good enough, you'll convict some people that their lives ought to be different. God give us churches and Christians that disturb people.

Spiritual Disturbance Is the Only Way to Genuine Peace

Spiritual disturbance is the only way to genuine peace. Martin Luther, that man of the Reformation who died with a peaceful heart, was not always at peace within. Only when he became disturbed about trying to go along with the Roman Church did he begin to find genuine peace. Because of his disturbance, he became a man of inner peace. Paul certainly died a man of peace. Before his death he said, "I have fought a good fight, I have finished my course, I have kept the faith: henceforth, there is laid up for me a crown of righteousness" (1 Tim. 4:7).

Paul died a man of peace. Why? Because when he was on the road to Damascus something came out of the sky and struck him blind. Paul's disturbance brought him lasting peace. What happened to Moses, who went into the mount to meet God, a man who knew tranquility and peace as only few ever knew? I'll tell you what happened to Moses. He had seen the burning bush; he heard the voice of God in heaven when he was attending the sheep of his father-in-law, Jethro. If Moses had never been disturbed, he would have never been a man of peace.

You'll never have peace in your life, genuine, wholesome, peace, until you are first of all disturbed about your lost, wayward condition. Sometimes a preacher comes to town and somebody says, "Oh, I don't like what he preached because he got our people all disturbed." We need more men who will get people disturbed about their lives.

You may remember a man by the name of Jonah. The Bible says that "Jonah was gone down into the sides of the ship;

and was fast asleep" (Jonah 1:5). The ship was rocking and the waves were tempestuous, slapping up against the sides of that vessel. Jonah realized God had caused the storm. He told the sailors, and Jonah was thrown overboard. A big fish came and swallowed him and later spit him upon dry land. Then he got back into the center of God's will.

The most dangerous time in the life of Jonah was when he was feeling that everything was OK. He was down in the bottom of the ship fast asleep, but not until the storm came was Jonah back into the will of God.

Have you had a storm in your life lately? If not, maybe you need one. We all need to be disturbed out of our lethargy. I hope that when my son goes to school that I'll be able to say to the school principal in all sincerity, "Sir, if that little fellow gets out of hand, discipline him. I'd rather him be disturbed now than to grow up and bring dishonor to me and to his mother and to his God."

I hope that when my son gets to be a teenager, I'll be able to say to the police officer, "Sir, if you catch my boy speeding; if you catch him out of line; if he is breaking the law, I hope you stop him. I hope you'll disturb him now and keep him from growing up and killing himself with wreckless driving upon the highways." Sometimes the greatest avenue to peace is first of all the pathway of disturbance. Are you disturbed about your life? Is there something in it that ought not to be?

I think all of us are familiar with the mobile x-ray units that come to our cities. What's the philosophy behind an x-ray unit? There's one philosophy—to stir people up. That's right. They come into a city with machines and get people to come by so they can take a picture of their lungs to see if they have cancer or tuberculosis. Sure enough they find people who never knew that they had cancer. The people are naturally worried and upset, but many of them prolong their life a year, five years, ten years, or even to a normal life because first of all, somebody got them upset. The truth that was disturbing led to healing that was delightful.

The Bible will often disturb, as will the cut of the physician's knife, but both lead to better days. Our lives must also be so Christlike that they may well disturb a decadent society, but that disturbance can be the vestibule of a beautiful sanctuary of peace.

11

When Heaven and Earth Meet

(Acts 14:8-18)

Out in West Texas and in Arizona especially, one can look as far as his eyes will allow him to see. As he gazes across the dry, arid, flat earth, he can see so very much sky and such a great deal of earth. In fact, he can see so much of it that he can see where the sky seems to be pouring down right upon the earth. This phenomenon of beauty has led many to comment, "Isn't it a beautiful sight to see heaven and earth meet?" And indeed it is!

Let us think about heaven and earth meeting, not in a visual illusion but in the terms of meaningful realities. Sometimes the eye of the heart sees with clearer and deeper vision than the eye of the head. So, with the eye of the heart we can see the power, direction, and glory of heaven, meeting with the needs, desires, and wonders of the earth. When does this meeting between heaven and earth take place?

As we read Acts 14:8-18, we see the developing drama of heaven meeting earth. As with viewing the scene in our western states, the meeting described here is also a source of beauty, splendor, and inspiration.

When Heaven and Earth Meet,
Men Are Made Whole

Paul came to a city and began to preach. A crippled man came to him. Paul preached to the man the gospel of Jesus Christ, and the man became whole. Now how did the man become whole? He didn't become whole when he jumped up and began to walk around. The man did not become cured when the people saw him running through their midst and shouting, "Look at me! Look what Paul has done! Look at what this God-come-to earth has done to me." That man was made whole when he first became whole *within*. I repeat, that man was not cured when he jumped to his feet. He was cured when he believed that he could jump to his feet. There is not any instance in the Bible in any of the books, when a man was ever healed only to make him physically whole. There was first of all a heart change.

In all instances in the Bible, men are healed because there is a spiritual lesson to be taught. And this is always an occasion when heaven comes down with its miraculous power to meet the great needs of the earth. There is no way for a man to be made whole unless first of all there is a meeting of heaven's power and earth's need.

The greatest healing of this man in this particular city was not that he "got feet," but that he "got heart." It was not that he was able to move swiftly among the people but that when the judgment day of God would come he could move swiftly into the kingdom of God. It wasn't that now he could speedily run and do the things that he needed to do but that he could lie down at night and have the peace of the Galilean in his soul.

That man might have been made to walk by some miracle of a surgeon's knife. That man could have been made to walk by some marvelous surgical procedure of advanced medicine, but the man would have still been unwhole. He still would have been only part man. You see, there are people today who need to be made whole who have absolutely not one physical disability. Now consider this spiritual lesson.

Look at this man—a cripple. Do you not know people in the world and do I not know people in the world today who are crippled because of their inactivity in God's work. Do

you not know people who need this kind of message that
says, "Come and be made whole"? There are some similarities
between a man who is physically cripple and one who is spiritually cripple.

For one thing, this man could not walk. From his birth
he could not walk. Now, the Bible doesn't say that he wasn't
living, but it says that he could not walk. Isn't that tragic?
He never could stand tall on his own two feet and place his
head up toward God and feel the breeze of God blowing
around him. He never could walk. Before Paul got this man
on his feet, he had to get him standing erect in his soul.

How many people do I know who have never walked? They
are breathing; they are existing; they are marking time; but
they have never walked. They've never been able to leap
for joy. They've never been able to run with the great ecstatic
joy that comes from knowing Jesus. They are breathing. They
are existing, but they are spiritual cripples. They have never
walked a step. What a tragic thing—men who cannot walk;
men who cannot get around on their own power; men who
are crippled spiritually. I know many of them. Maybe some
of them sit in churches every Sunday. They are crawling, they
never have walked, stood erect, and been proud of their lives.

Notice another similarity between physical and spiritual
cripples. The physically crippled is inevitably dependent upon
somebody else. Do you think this crippled man stayed in the
same spot all of his life? Oh, no. How did he get around?
He was dependent upon somebody who was whole.

One of the popular pastimes in our world today is to hammer
away at the foundation of the church. Yet, the message of
the church is the only real help for the crippled people of
the world: the lost, the drunkard, the idolater, the playboy.
People are wholly dependent upon the church for their walking. What a tragedy it is that the evil people of the world,
who would take us out of existence, are living today in the
freedom of America because of the church of Jesus Christ.

Every crippled man is dependent upon somebody else. The only way America is marching forward, the only reason we are going any place, the only reason we have any moral sanity at all, is because of the good people who are whole—who are able to carry the morally crippled people on their backs. The church and its message of Christ are the health in an otherwise sick body.

These are two qualities of the crippled man. First of all—he exists, but he will never really walk. Second of all, he is dependent upon somebody else. And now the third, nobody wants to look at him. Yet, the church (as did Paul) is willing to look at the needs of the world and heal the broken lives. I want to ask the world why it wants to slap the hand that helps, holds, and heals. We will never find our world any less crippled than it is until the world learns that it is dependent upon the Lord of heaven for every good thing it enjoys. It is a shame how many illustrations can be found to indicate the number of people who are crippled in their souls.

I shall never forget an experience I had in Colorado Springs. I had to take a young boy to his home. When we went into the house, a baby was crying. I went into the baby's room and in the baby bed, a small infant lay. I said to the young boy, "Where is your mother and dad?"

He said, "Well, Daddy is in Germany. Mother's out dancing with another man."

"Who's taking care of the baby?" I asked.

"Nobody, nobody."

"The baby's crying, don't you want to pick it up? Don't you want to clutch it to your chest? Don't you want to give it a bottle? Don't you want to keep it from crying?" I said.

"No, it will be all right. It will be all right. Mother will be back before daylight," came his reply.

In our world today, there are some people so crippled that if you looked on them, you would get sick. This crippled man in Acts, first of all, had to be made whole inside before he could ever walk. When heaven and earth meet, it's a time when men are made whole.

When Heaven and Earth Meet, Men Are Godly

After Paul healed the crippled man, the people ran to Paul and Barnabas, believing them to be gods. They called Barnabas one god and Paul another god. They thought, "My, this is a mighty thing; these gods have come in flesh." They wanted to make sacrifices to them, but Paul and Barnabas would not allow it. Paul and Barnabas rent their clothes and ran out among the people, saying, "Why do you do these things? We also are men of like passions with you" (Acts 14:15).

Paul and Barnabas were more; they were godly men. Look at some of the evidence of their godliness. *They were honest men.* They could have said, "Yes, you're right. We are two of the gods," and exploited the people. Isn't that a tragic thing, though, when a man sets himself up as a god? When heaven and earth meet, it inevitably meets in the heart of a godly man.

Wives, do you consider your husbands godly men? Father, do you consider that you are a godly father for your children? Of all of the particular words that could be used to describe you, would one be godly? Are you that close to God? Paul and Barnabas were so close to God that when they were getting credit for really being God, they refused to take it. *They were honest men.*

They were also humble men. They could have reacted many ways. They could have really boasted about being gods. Paul could have said, "Look at the miracle that I have done." But Paul was able to say, "It was God who did it. I'm a man just like you are a man." Paul was an humble man.

Have you ever known anybody who just couldn't stand not getting all of the recognition he wanted? Someday I'm going to preach a sermon on the sin of getting your feelings hurt. One of the greatest curses upon the church is when people have to walk so carefully in order not to upset somebody else. It's a headache to the pastor, to the music director, to the educational direction, and the Sunday School teachers when they have to walk on thin ice, afraid that somebody might get upset. If some people are like that, they are not like Paul and Barnabas. They're not humble people. For an humble person says, "I do my work to the glory and praise of God." And if you don't do it for that, it would be better not doing it at all.

Isn't it awful that some people have to be prodded and pulled in order to get them to do what God wants them to do? I wonder what kind of help you are to your Sunday School teacher. Do you make her job easier? Or do you make it harder? Do you cause him to visit you when he could be visiting somebody in much worse shape?

When we are dedicated to God, heaven and earth meet and all of the blessings and riches of God's heaven can be poured in upon man's need and there can be great service for God. Paul and Barnabas were godly men for they did what God wanted them to do. God works through the men like that. That's where heaven meets earth—in godly men.

When Men Are Willing to See God in Their World, Heaven and Earth Meet

As Paul preached to these people, he was so discouraged because they only saw God in him. The people were thinking to themselves, "If Paul and Barnabas are not Mercury and Jupiter, then is there a god around? They must surely be gods." Paul said, "No, we are not God, but God has not left you without a witness—the witness of himself."

Paul and Barnabas could see God in the sunshine. They could see God in the sun that would glisten on the dew and make the world look like it was carpeted with silver. They could see God in the song of the robin. They could see God in the very beautiful grass that covers the pastureland. They could see God in the setting of the sun. They could see God in the rain. They could see God through the fragrance of the flower.

Paul said, God "left not himself without a witness, in that he did good, and gave us rain from heaven, and fruitful seasons, filling our hearts with food and gladness" (Acts 14:17). He's an awfully ignorant man who cannot see God in the universe. The difference between man and animals is so vast that you have to know that man was created not in the image of the monkey but in the image of God. Some people enjoy telling us of all of the similarities between the ape and the man (and there are similarities). But there are more similarities between man and God than there are between man and animal. Genesis says that man was made in the image of God (see 1:26-27). That doesn't mean that God has hands. It doesn't mean that God has eyes and ears and feet and legs. It means man was made in the spiritual image of God. We don't even know if God has a body. God is Spirit.

So God made us like the monkeys—some of us more than others. What if God made us with fingers and hands and with eyes and ears like the animals, so what? That's the way he wanted our bodies to be, but it doesn't mean that we are made in their likeness, for we are made in the spiritual likeness of God.

Have you ever considered the great differences? Have you ever watched a baboon sit on a tree admiring the beautiful sunrise? Have you ever read a poem written by a kangaroo about a dandelion? Have you ever watched a dog stand on a porch and just be amazed at the beautiful ecstatic beauty of the universe? No! Why? Because even though physically there are some similarities—animals have hearts, but they do not have souls, and the soul is that which perceives. The soul is that which gives a sense of beauty. That is a witness of God. The way he made you and me is so different from the way he made animals; there is not one spiritual similarity.

Not only that, but God left the witness of his Word. His book with 66 books, 1189 chapters, 31,173 verses, every one of them inspired by God, has never been outsold by day, week, month, or year since the first printing of the Bible. It has withstood every onslaught of Communism, atheism, and agnosticism that the world has ever been able to give. The Bible is a witness of the truth of God.

The church of Jesus Christ is another witness. I'm so amazed at some of our little fuzzy-faced high school students who get off to college. They hear some professor say something contrary to the Word of God and begin to believe him. Isn't that an amazing thing? Some little, immature, adolescent hears what a foolish professor says and it begins to shake his faith.

My friend, you tell that professor that the church of Jesus Christ was here a thousand years before he was ever born and it will be here a thousand years after he is gone and forgotten. You tell him that he is temporal. You tell him that this is celestial. The witnesses of God are vast.

When does earth meet heaven? They meet when men are made whole; when whole men help crippled men to become whole men. They meet when there is miraculous performing of the Word of God and men are made godly. Heaven meets earth when men are willing to see God in their world.

12

Detained but Not Defeated

(Acts 14:19-28)

Life undoubtedly has its disenchantments, disappointments, and disillusionments, and certainly some detainments, but a life that is rightly related to God can be a life that can never know defeat. Occasions come when life seems to be at its end; when we think that to go on isn't really worth the trouble. Because of the disadvantages, because of the heartache and the disappointments, because of the many impediments and various obstacles in life, some wonder, why make the effort?

The child of God can say that, even though life for him must have its detainments, life for him can never know defeat if he truly has the proper perspective. One of the greatest works ever penned by man took the author three years of meticulous effort to accomplish. He gave the original manuscript to a man friend to read, and the friend left the manuscript on his desk. While he was gone his house burned. In the tragic loss of all his possessions, the friend of the famous author also lost the manuscript that had taken three years to compose.

You can imagine, since the author had no other copy, what he felt when he was told by his friend how sorry he was that the manuscript was burned. The man wondered to himself, "What can I do? I surely could never be inspired to write like that again. What can I do?" He began with the first word, the first page, the first chapter and wrote it all over again. And when his friend read the second manuscript he said to himself, "Well, what part of the original one I read, the second one certainly is superior to the first." Here is a secular example of a man who was detained in the pivotal work that he wanted to accomplish, but he was not defeated.

Whether in life you are simply detained or whether you are genuinely defeated does not depend upon the circumstance of your life, but it depends on you.

In Acts 14 we find this drama of the apostle Paul who was detained in his work, but by the grace and the power of his commitment, he was never defeated. We will look at verses 19-28. Whether your life is going to be a life of detainment or a life of defeat may depend on how you answer the following questions.

Is Your Dedication More Powerful than Pain?

Ask yourself these questions, Will my life be full of detainments or defeat? Is my dedication more powerful than pain? Do I ever think about what God has meant for my life? As you ponder these questions, you'll determine whether your life will be one of defeat or whether it will simply be one of detours, disappointments, detainments, and postponements.

When you ask the question, Is my commitment to the cause of Jesus Christ more powerful than pain? you certainly ask yourself a big question. When Paul came to the city of Lystra, I have an idea he preached the same gospel that he had preached in Antioch of Pisidia. He preached the same gospel he had preached outside the city of Jerusalem. He preached the same gospel he had preached the first time he had opened his mouth to that congregation of Jews. He preached the sovereignty and the elective power of God. He preached the justification of man through the power of the cross. He preached the sanctification of the saints. He preached the endurance of people who came to know Jesus Christ. He preached the gospel.

Paul actually was not surprised when the stoning began. I

believe with all of my heart that Paul knew those stones were going to be thrown at him. Now he had a lot of options. Paul could have said to himself, Now, there is no use getting killed because God doesn't want us to kill ourselves in his service. After all, I can get down from here and mean a lot more to the kingdom of God alive. Instead, he preached Jesus more. He preached that there was salvation only in the God of Abraham, Isaac, and Jacob. He preached that the only way home is the way of the cross. He preached that there is no other way to God outside of Jesus Christ.

The stones began to come. I imagine even little children, who were influenced by their parents, probably threw stones. Probably some did not hit vital parts of his body at first, and Paul preached with more faith and determination and enthusiasm. The stones began to strike his chest and his arms and his legs, and some even sneaked up behind him and hit the back of his head with all of their might. Paul continued to preach. Paul uttered a word for Christ as some great stone crushed him in the mouth and blood began to gush from his gums and his teeth were loosened from his mouth. Even through the blood and grit, I imagine that Paul muttered the good news.

Paul kept on preaching and finally, they beat him to such a pulp that he fell to the ground. The ground around him was stained with his blood. His clothing—you could hardly see a spot on it that wasn't red. The people dragged him by the feet out of the city. And I can imagine as they dragged him across that street with his head bumping upon the stones, his hair snagged on a twig sticking up from the earth. Somebody must have come over to him and thrown a rock down on his face again. Somebody placed his sandal on Paul's nose and twisted his foot in Paul's face as if stamping out a cigarette. They dragged him out of the city and left him, brushed off their hands, and marched back into the city as if they had done their religious duty.

His friends were upset, for the tongue of Paul had been stopped. The voice of faith and contentment and love and salvation was now silenced. So they gathered around Paul and somebody said to somebody else, "Go get a piece of wood if you will." Somebody said, "Go get a metal scraper." They gathered around him, I suppose, to bury him. They were about to have his funeral. But Paul had a big surprise waiting for them. He sat up. Now some scholars think Paul was dead and he was resurrected. The Bible doesn't say either way. It says, "they supposed him to be dead." If Paul were dead enough to convince his enemies that he was dead, maybe he was. Maybe he had a true resurrection by the power and grace of God. It could have been, but that's not important.

Teachers and preachers, what would you do if someone told you next Sunday if you taught your lesson you would be stoned? What would you do if somebody told you that if you witnessed to a particular man, he would stone you until you were bloody and throw you outside of his house and leave you on the street to die? This is when you ask the question, Is my commitment more significant than my desire to escape pain?

Let us never think that if it's an inconvenience to us to do something for God, we have the right to give up. It does not! If being inconvenienced for the sake of Jesus Christ causes you to quit working for Christ, I doubt seriously that the apostle would ever agree with you that you know the one called Jesus. When a man is stoned and beaten and can go right back into the city, something vital is in his life.

We'll never have defeated pastors, we'll never have defeated church workers if we are people who say, "My commitment is stronger than my desire to escape pain." Paul had a reason to live. Paul said, "For me to live is Christ, and to die is gain." He was saying, "I can't be defeated," and surely he wasn't. Let's make Christ our all—that is real Christianity.

Ask yourself the question, Is my desire to please God more

important than my desire to escape pain? If it is, I want you
to notice something about Paul, as he got up and returned
into the city (v. 20). Paul put the emphasis of his life on the
difficult. This is hard to do; it's hard for me to do and it's
hard for you to do. I repeat, Paul put his greatest emphasis
on the difficult. Do you think that Paul got up from those
stones and from that puddle of blood and marched back into
that city singing, "Onward Christian Soldiers"? I don't think
so.

Courage is never easy. Faith is never frivolous. I think Paul
got up from that great mass of blood and anguish with torn
flesh hanging from his cheeks. His nose was broken and only
a few teeth were still left in his head. He marched back into
that city wondering just what was going to happen. Paul knew
though that a Christian gives his best at his most difficult hour.
The most difficult time Paul ever had was at Lystra. He never
got stoned again. Twenty years later, Paul said in one of his
epistles, "once was I stoned." He remembered it. It happened
at Lystra, but he went back.

Have you ever thought about that—putting the emphasis
of your life on the difficult? If your difficulty is faithfulness,
you ought to try harder at that point. If your difficulty is stinginess with God's money, you ought to emphasize that point
instead of saying, "I do good over here, therefore, I can do
bad in this area." If your difficulty is that you don't like to
visit, that's more the reason you ought to visit. The hardest
area, where the stones are roughest, where the crowds are
most difficult, *is where we might need to spend most of our
time.* We'll never build a greater Christianity if people just
go down the path of least resistance, down the avenues that
they can travel without ditches, without bumps, without
curves, and without hills. We'll never do anything until people
say, "Where my weakness is, there I'll put my greatest effort."
Paul knew that where there are stones there is great possibility
of victorious witness. And he went back.

What's your greatest problem? Your tongue? Then you need to do something about that. Put your greatest emphasis there. You don't go to church on Sunday night? You can't make up for it on Sunday morning. Make a commitment to be more faithful to your church.

What if a carpenter came to my house and said, "I'm real good with hammering, but there's only one thing I can't do—saw."

What if I said, "Well, go ahead anyway." He works and he hammers on the boards, with one of them six feet out this way, one of them is three feet over that way, and one of them is four and one-half inches sticking out here. They're crooked and jagged because he could hammer well, but he couldn't saw.

Or, if a plumber came to your house and said, "I can do well digging the ditch," and he digs the ditch, but he can't put the pipes together and you have leaks.

Or, what would a church do with a preacher they called and he said, "Now, I like to visit the hospitals and I like to visit people in their homes, but I just can't do this preaching. It's difficult for me to prepare three sermons a week, therefore, I'm not going to do it." A church wouldn't call him.

Christians must start emphasizing the things that are hardest for them to do. That's what Paul was willing to do because he thought more of his dedication to God than he did of enduring a little bit of pain. Yes, I know we must work most in the area of our spiritual gifts, but the point remains—we must be willing to adapt and work with diligence in areas that might be difficult for us.

Is My Life Governed by the Fact That God Has Blessed Me?

One cannot be defeated if he knows that God loves him and blesses him, is within him, cares for him, directs him, and guides him. If one has as his prime motivation to show appreciation for what God has done for him, then that man will always be a victor.

Think about creation. God made the animals, the vegetables, the sea and the air, the light and darkness, and he said they were good. But when he made man, God said he was *very* good.

What happened in the Garden of Eden when Adam sinned and was found naked? Did God come to Adam and Eve and say, "What you need is more apples; what you need is more fruit trees; what you need is better housing; what you need is a greater social care"? No. God said they needed a covering for *their* nakedness. To many God's act of covering them stands as a symbol of the atoning work of Christ. The greatest thing God has done for us is not let us have the comforts of the world, but rather to send Jesus Christ to die on the cross for us. We no longer are bound for an eternal hell, but we are bound for heaven. Praise God for that! Have you thought about the cross lately?

Read on in Acts 14, "And when they were come, and had gathered the church together, they rehearsed all that God had done with them, and how he had opened the door of faith unto the Gentiles" (v. 27). You see, when you're talking about the grace of God, the stones don't matter. The blood couldn't matter less. The scars, the hurt, the sacrifice, and the pain are really of no significance if you are rehearsing all that God has done with you. Our blessings are so numerous.

While many of us are fussing because we do not have particular kinds of food, there are people in this land who are scraping the bottoms of garbage cans to exist. While some of you teenagers are pestering your mothers and fathers because you can't have some more clothes, there are teenagers in this world who would give anything for their first new clothes. While we would love to have a better pair of shoes, there are people without feet who will never leave their crutches because of their deformities. While some people would love to have better automobiles, there are people in this world who have never been in one and they go everywhere on beasts of burden. Have you counted your blessings? Are you rehearsing what God has done?

When I think of Paul lying there in that street with his life almost gone (possibly it was), I wonder what spurred Paul to get up and go back into Lystra? I think he got up not only to help those people to be saved but also Paul must have said to himself, Oh, what's my life worth if it's not worth something for Jesus? You see, Paul was willing to realize what God had done and, he was willing to do something more for God.

Think of the future God gives us. Have you read the Scripture that says when Christ comes, "we shall all be changed, in a moment, in a twinkling of an eye" (1 Cor. 15:51-52). Do you know what that word "change" means in Greek? "Metamorphosis." You shall be "metamorphosis" in a moment, in a twinkling of an eye. Have you ever seen a cocoon? It's an ugly thing you don't want to touch. You don't want to look at it. Nobody would ever enlarge a colored picture of it and put it on his wall. But what happens after metamorphosis? The worm in the cocoon becomes a beautiful butterfly. It's gorgeous. Its colors give us some aesthetic pleasure as we look at it. A complete metamorphosis, a complete change has taken place.

It's going to happen to you and me. One day there's going to be metamorphosis; one day we are going to be changed and what really now is a cocoon existence is going to bloom in heaven as a butterfly. This life is relative to heaven but only as a beginning of what the true blossoming life will really be. Isn't that a beautiful thought to know? The best life we are going to have is still out yonder. We are still as a cocoon to a butterfly in comparing this life to our heavenly life.

Have you rehearsed what God has done for you? If you have, you cannot be mediocre any more. Those of you barely related to the church, those of you hanging on to its skirts at a distance, I ask you to dedicate your lives fully to Jesus. Those of you who should teach, fill places of responsibility, or take places of leadership, do it now. What more does God have to do to awaken you to deep service? Some of you with talents, with means, with abilities—God has blessed you, but you're not using his blessings in his service. What if God should take them away from you? You would probably be disappointed with God. Use them for him. God will bless you as he has never blessed you before.

Let me ask you, Do you live a defeated life or a detained one? The answer to that question is determined by how you answer these questions: Am I willing to be more dedicated than I am to fear pain? Do I really live a life of gratitude to God? Those who stand for Christ and his righteousness may be detained, as Paul was at Lystra, but never defeated.

13
Walking in the Sunlight

(Acts 15:1-35)

Christianity has too long been identified with somber words, music, and attitudes. While some of Christianity's worship ought to be sedate, much of it I'm afraid, might even be senile. Too much of Christianity has become bland.

This regrettable emphasis influences what is expected of the Christian minister. We expect him to wear a black suit, black tie, black socks, and probably would be shocked if we knew some of his breed had red polka-dots on their pajamas. When my wife and I decided to buy a new car, I suggested that instead of getting one that looked like one a preacher would buy, we should get a pretty one.

Christianity was not meant to be a sterile, harmless cause in the world. It was meant to shake people and awaken them. People should leave our services eager to do something daring for the cause of Christ. This is why I like our worship services to have the assistance of a trumpet and a drum or two. I feel like the Salvation Army marching song probably gets deeper into the heart of Christianity than some sleepy choir struggling through a German chorale.

Christianity, then, is a faith that belongs in the sunshine. It is bright. It is springtime fresh. It's refreshing as the morning dew. Never dull, dry, drab, or boring is the cause of the exciting Christ.

In the story of the first Christian council meeting found in Acts 15:1-32, the truth of Christianity's sunshine approach to life is spelled out. The early followers of our Lord were saying that the Christian faith has jumped from the damp, dark shadows to the brilliant beams of sunlight. As Christians, we walk in the sunshine.

Christians Do Not Walk in the Shadow of Historical Hebraism

At the time of the first Christian council, there was a great deal of discussion between the conservatives and liberals. There were some of the people who believed if you belong to God, you had to do exactly like the people long ago had to do. You had to undergo all of the ceremonies, all of the pomp, all of the great acts of ritualism that so described the original Hebrew synagogue, the Temple worship, and the worship even in the wilderness.

Therefore, the conservative Pharisees were upset when they heard that one could be saved through the power of Jesus Christ. They had never thought about that, for they were still under the shadow of ceremonial law, still under the shadow of the religion of Moses, still under the shadow of ancient codes and laws that were as outdated as anything could possibly be.

You see, there is a great deal of difference between Judaism and Christianity. And while we will have to admit that Christianity has some overtones of Judaism today, Christianity came into the world to fulfill the law and not to be under it. It was to bring the law up to date. Today as Christians, you and I are no longer under the shadow of historical Hebraism.

The Jew forgot that while outward signs of religion were basically good, there were inherent dangers. The danger is this. When a person uses the outward symbol for his religion, he finds himself worshiping the symbol instead of that which the symbol represents. The Jews never learned that. Prayer for them was not talking to God but merely a part of what they had to do. For them, prayer was a routine. For them, religion was simply a part of life instead of the pattern for life.

One of the ancient Jews, as the story goes, was chasing a man in order to kill him. He had his dagger drawn behind his head ready to plunge into the back of his victim. All of a sudden he looked up at the sun and noticed that it was time to pray. So he took his blanket from beneath his robe and placed it out on the ground, kneeled into the street, bowed his knee upon the blanket and prayed unto Jehovah God. He then got up from his place and continued with his plan to commit murder.

Now this sounds silly and ridiculous to us. The overtones of this kind of religion still exist in Christendom today. There are still a large group of people that, for some reason or another, put religion here, business there, habits here, pleasures there, and activities here. Religion has a place in their lives, but it has never changed them.

Christianity says that we are not living under the shadow of historical Hebraism. We are living under the sunlight. We are living under a new code, under a new law that says we have freedom, absolute freedom from the law. To be under grace means to be under love. That freedom is one of the most confining freedoms you can know. For who wants to hurt the love of God. Who wants to prostitute the grace of God by one day following God and the next day living like the devil? Christianity was meant as a way and a form of life.

Jesus Christ said, in some of his parables, Christianity is not to be a new patch on the old garment of Hebraism. For when that garment is washed you will find one piece of material pulling against the other and because of the shrinkage there will be a tear. He said, "Neither do men put new wine into old bottles: else the bottles break." Christianity is not under the shadow of ceremonialism; it is a new way of life altogether.

Do you know that there is a direct correlation between

liturgical worship and teaching about abstention? Liturgical worship generally means high church where the preachers wear their ecclesiastical garb, people go through various ritualistic activities, where there are parades up and down the aisles with men dressed in their ancient attire and carrying decorated banners.

I repeat, there is a direct correlation between liturgical worship and the lack of teaching against abstention. Why is that so? Because when people have too many objects to represent God, they believe that when the object has been paid homage, God can be forgotten. Now that is not always intentional, but it can happen. That's why if you will go to some of the most liturgical of Christian bodies in the world, you will often find the greatest liberalism. In fact, one of the liturgical priests wrote in a sexually-oriented magazine sometime ago why it was all right for two agreeing parties to have sexual relations before marriage. The further you go toward strong liturgical worship, the more permissiveness you find.

I see a danger point in my own denomination. If we keep going toward high church services, if we keep going toward music that people like because they think it is intellectually edifying instead of Christ uplifting, if we go to sermons that are pretty but sterile, then we are going to find ourselves also separating worship from our lives. That gives opportunity to edit the Bible instead of obeying the Bible.

Take a look at the Pentecostal groups. They are people who have a more simple form of worship. You will discover in their lives and in their testimonies a form of Christianity that will put most Baptist people absolutely to shame. Why? Because they have not put obstacle after obstacle in their path. They have a desire to have direct access to the Holy Spirit and to God, and they don't care about formal stuff just so they can worship and say, "I've done my religion."

One can worship every kind of form in the world and go to hell, but you have to worship Jesus Christ in order to go to heaven. We've become church worshipers; we've become worship worshipers; and we've become music worshipers instead of worshipers of Christianity.

There's a great danger in Christianity today. Hinting at this danger, Peter said something like, "Why do you want those people to be bound by something that the Jews can't even live up to?" (see Acts 15:10). Paul and Barnabas continued with a different kind of logic. They said something like: "Look at all of these Gentiles who have been saved. Look at them over here who have been converted. Look at them north, south, east, and west who have been born again. They've never heard about your Jewish faith. They don't know about all of your ceremonies. They don't know about your ritualism" (see Acts 15:12). You see, Paul and Barnabas gave the greatest testimony for the cause of Jesus Christ, that he can change a life completely.

Mark 7 records a confrontation Jesus had with religious leaders. They were concerned because the disciples were not ceremonially cleaning their hands (this was done by putting an egg shell and a half of water and letting it run from their elbows down to the tip of their fingers). They didn't care if the disciples hands were clean or not; they were not ceremonially clean if they didn't at least go through the act of worship and ceremony. Jesus called them hypocrites. The Greek word that Jesus used is *hupokrites*. It was the word that was used for the play actor. The actor playing the part of a clown might put a mask on his face that had a smile on it; *hupokrite*, but on the inside behind this wooden mask the actor might be frowning.

A paraphrase of Jesus' speech might be: "You religious Pharisees are just like that. You *hupokrites*. You put on a mask, but as soon as you walk out of the church door, you close the door upon your religion. It's more important that the disciples really have clean hands than have ceremonially clean hands." Today it's more important that our preachers and

122

Real Christianity

our people be pure in life, pure in body, pure in heart, pure in everything, than that they come to Sunday School and Church Training and fork over the dollar. Too many forget that Christianity is not a matter of churchism or religiosity; it's a matter of the inner man. This is Christian faith. This is walking in the sunlight.

We Are Not Under the Shadow of Personal Pursuits

Now we find this most refreshing passage of Scripture, "For it seemed good to the Holy Ghost, and to us, to lay upon you no greater burden than these necessary things" (Acts 15:28). Oh, if that could be said about the church. That should be said about all of our business dealings; it should be said about our preachers and our leaders—it seemed "good to the Holy Ghost and to us."

Am I able to say that wherever I am found, I am there because it seemed good to me and to the Holy Spirit? Oh, that would change the life of every church. It would change the life of our people if we had the courage and conviction enough to say, when it becomes pleasing to the Holy Spirit, it becomes pleasing to me.

Christians often say, "But I like to do it." Is that really the issue? "But I've always done it." That's what Christ is supposed to change—you, your personality, your faults. You can never fall back on that excuse, "That's just me, that's just the way I am." If that's the way you are, you ought to be different. Christianity comes to take us from the shadow of personal pursuits. We no longer seek things after our own desires, our tastes, our pleasures, our ambitions, our thoughts; we seek things according to God's law—the Holy Spirit.

If you were to touch a pail of water that had an electric node in it, you probably would not get your finger wet at all; but immediately you would sense the electricity that was flowing through the water. If you were to touch an iron rod that had been in a furnace, you couldn't tell me what kind of metal it was because of the intense heat that was there. You could only feel the heat. And when people come in contact with my life and with your life, they ought not to touch us, but they ought to touch something warmer. They should touch God. He ought to be so full in our lives that when I'm touched and when you're touched, others don't even know who we are, but they know they've been close to God.

My father worked for the Dallas Railway Company for many years. He was working there when I was born. He drove a streetcar, a train-looking vehicle, that ran on tracks down the middle of the streets of Dallas, transporting people to and fro from work to home. He had a phrase that he would often use—"skinning the wire." When he would pull on a handle, the trolley above the streetcar would barely touch the wire that was above and he would slow down. That was "skinning the wire." When he would push the trolley handle away that trolley would come down more firmly on the wire and the streetcar would speed up because it rested more heavily on the source of power.

We need our lives more firmly upon our source of power, which is the Holy Spirit. We must pray, read our Bible, and attend church faithfully. No one can grow strong by eating once a week. I usually eat three meals if I can't eat four or five. We ought to go to church, pray, witness, and study the Word to get our spiritual strength.

Christians must realize that we are no longer under the shadow of personal pursuits. I read something one time that I think is significant: "Unless there is within us that which is above us, we had better be careful then, about that which is around us." Are you being influenced too much by that which is around you because within you there is not much of that which is above you? There are some battles that you cannot fight by yourself. There has to be something from above.

Walking in the Sunlight Also Means That the Christian Does Not Walk in the Shadow of Irrational Living

"For it seemed good to the Holy Ghost, and to us, to lay upon you no greater burden than these necessary things" (Acts 15:28). Notice what these "necessary things" were. "That you abstain from meats offered to idols, and from blood, and from things strangled, and from fornication: from which if ye keep yourselves, ye shall do well" (v. 29). And then he says good-bye, "Fare ye well," is the way the King James Version has it.

To abstain from meat offered to idols and from blood was not a Hebrew law, it was a civil law. That law was placed in the Old Testament before Moses was ever born. This was not a law of religion. It was a law of the state. Therefore, those preachers of Christ were telling the new converts that when they came by grace, through Jesus Christ, to do two things: to be obedient to the law by abstaining from things strangled, from tasting of blood and to be free from sexual sin. If the converts did those two things, Paul said, "Ye shall do well."

Christians who know what the Bible teaches have always been obedient to the laws of the land. All of us have our problem at this point. Every Christian who knows what the Bible says knows it teaches us to be obedient to the law. Some hecklers tried to trick Jesus in this area one time. He looked at those criticizers and said, "Render therefore unto Caesar the things which are Caesar's; and unto God the things that are God's." They questioned the apostle Paul one time because the Christians wanted to do something out of hand. Paul wrote them, and the first thing he told them was, "Be obedient to the laws of the land for they will do us good."

Our government is good to us. If the government were to tax our total properties, you and I would be out of a lot of things. We would be in a terrible shape. A Christian is to be a sane, sensible person. Christianity never made an idiot out of anyone. We are to be obedient to the law. Christianity no longer walks under the shadow of irrational living. This is why I can't understand why some of our so-called intellectuals have difficulty with Christianity. It's the most sensible thing in all of the world.

Just recently I cut out an article from the newspaper. The headline reads: "Parliament of India Burst into Uproar over the Holy Cow Issue." The first paragraph says, "With an indignant howl of outrage the Indian Parliament broke into an uproar Thursday when the minister of food suggested that the Holy Cow had been eaten as a delicacy in the Vedic Era about three thousand years ago." And the people got so upset that the crowd jumped up and screamed and said, "Send him to Pakistan, get him out of the country."

Hinduism is letting thousands and millions of people starve. India has a higher starvation rate than China does today. And yet, cows roam the streets and stores because the religion of the land says, "Do not eat it."

If you're a Christian, you're not under the shadow of irrational living. Some of the habits that are against the Word of God, in which you are engaged, are bringing unhappiness in your life. I promise you that you will be unhappy in your eternity unless you come back to the complete Word of God. The most rational, sensible, solid thing that a man can do is to be Christian in all of his life.

What's the shadow you're under? If you are walking in darkness today, under some shadow, your step is out of the step of God. For when you walk with Jesus, you do not walk under the shadow of vague, senseless, ritualism. You do not walk under the shadow of petty pleasures, but you're disciplined by something else all the time. When you are walking in the sunlight, you walk in the most sensible, solid way in which a man can walk—the way of Jesus Christ.

14

How to Rear a Missionary

(Acts 16:1-4)

Some people believe that a person is largely the product of his circumstances. This is especially true in the home. A child reflects the home in which he was reared. After all, the reason there are little monkeys is because the mothers and daddies were monkeys.

I have noticed this influence in extreme cases. For instance, I remember as a young native of Dallas, Texas, reading the life story of our hometown hero, Doak Walker. His father was so intent on young Doak becoming a football player that he had the boy kicking and throwing a football almost the day he could walk. He had him practice kicking the ball over the clothesline in the backyard. And sure enough he achieved greatness.

Another such story is of Mickey Mantle, whose father was just as concerned that Mickey play baseball as Doak's father was that his son play football. So, here are two cases which illustrate what I am saying. Parents can have a great deal to do with the values and aspirations of their children. Of course, the examples of even more notable cases would run into the millions.

This being true, let us ask ourselves what we are putting into the lives of children to determine their future. Are our homes Christian enough that maybe a preacher could be reared from our home? Or maybe a missionary? This usually takes more than an average mediocre home. It takes a home that is genuinely deep and sincere about the great work that God has for men and women to do. It takes a home of real Christianity.

In the book of Acts we are told of such a home. It was Timothy's home. His mother, Eunice, and his grandmother, Lois, provided an atmosphere in which a missionary could be reared. Would you like to have a son like Timothy? Want to rear a missionary? Oh, I don't necessarily mean one who goes across the seas, but at least one that is bone-deep a Christian and daily active in the work of the Lord.

Help Him to Love and Stay
Close to the Book of Books

In 2 Timothy 3:15, we read, "From a child thou has known the holy scriptures." If there were any one influential thing in the life of the young missionary Timothy, it was that he learned and appreciated and was associated with the holy Scripture. Surely it must be significant to us that Timothy's formative life was shaped and molded around Scripture.

Can't you look at this young man, Timothy, and imagine how mentally he camped at the riverside with the Israelites? He ran up once to the Red Sea and saw the water there, but all of a sudden because of the great work of God, it parted. He walked up Mount Sinai with Moses and heard the voice of God. He saw the fire on the mountainside. He walked down it with Moses. Can't you see young Timothy as he walked with Abraham, who by faith was looking for a city whose builder and maker was God? Can't you see young Timothy, in all of the vigor and vitality and vim of his young life, walking with Joshua around the walls of Jericho, watching those walls fall? Can't you see him standing with Ezekiel in the valley of the dry bones when all of a sudden the voice of God came and those bones began to join joint to joint and flesh came upon the bones and they began to speak? Can't you imagine young Timothy in the den of lions, scared to death for his young friend Daniel? Then his mother read, "My God hath sent his angel, and hath shut the lions' mouths," and what a joy came in that young heart.

Can't you see him in the belly of the whale with Jonah? His mother may not have finished the story that night and little Timothy may have gone to bed wondering what the results were going to be. And can't you see him with Isaiah who wept at the death of King Uzziah? Can't you see him preaching with Amos, crying, "Let judgment run down as waters"? Can't you see young Timothy hear the repentant psalmist say, "I sought the Lord, and he heard me, and delivered me from all my fears"? What do you think young Timothy must have thought when his mother read from Proverbs the words of Solomon, "As vinegar to the teeth, as smoke to the eyes, so is the sluggard to them that send him" (Prov. 10:26).

When he read in the Bible about Jacob talking Esau out of his birthright, he learned the tragic truth of life—some men are willing to sell their most important possessions for one moment of pleasure. All men need to realize that so they can avoid that pitfall.

Did not he learn when he read the story of David and Goliath (or when it was read to him) that if a man's heart is right with God, the giants of the world will always fall before him? Didn't he learn when David stood before Goliath that when a man is rightly related with the work of God then, and only then, does he become a big man? The truly big men of the world are men who are true with God.

Don't you think when somebody read to him about how Hosea forgave Gomer because God told him to that Timothy learned something about the forgiveness of God? That's a mighty lesson indeed.

Can you imagine then, with all of the adventures of the Old Testament a part of Timothy's life, how he could help but be different? Do you want to rear a missionary in your home? Help him to love the Book; help him to love the Word; help him to know the Bible more than he knows you or anything else in the world.

Abraham Lincoln's mother made a tremendous statement when she was asked about her son becoming president of the United States. She said, "I would rather Abe Lincoln know the Bible than to own the biggest farm in Pennsylvania and to be the president of the whole world." What a wise statement.

This Bible, this Book, how badly our young people need to be taught it. Webster said that "a man who has been through a thousand high schools and universities and does not know the Bible is not an educated man."

Would it honor your home to have some young lady, some young man leave that place familiar to him to go to a distant shore to tell about Jesus? Go ahead, parent, buy him a car if you can afford it. But don't forget to tell him that the greatest companion of traveling is the Word of God. Send him to a university if you will, the best one that your pocketbook can afford, but don't ever forget that if your child becomes the most educated man in the world and he is ignorant of the knowledge of God's Word, he is a fool. For the fool saith in his heart, "There is no God." Tell your child about all that's lovely in life. Let him subscribe to the magazine he enjoys, but don't ever forget to tell him unless he subscribes to what God has taught, all of his pleasures and habits and hobbies and fun are absolutely useless.

Surround Him with the Best Christians You Know

Do you want to rear a missionary for Jesus? Surround your child with the best Christians you know. Paul talked incessantly about Eunice and Lois. He talked of their unfeigned, undaunted faith. How he loved them. Often Paul and Barnabas, in the heat of the day, might have stopped by the house of this lovely mother, Eunice, and lovely grandmother, Lois, and found inspiration as they talked about the great work of God in the Old Testament and how God had sent the Messiah in the person of Jesus Christ.

But Timothy's home was not a home without its trouble. There was a man living in that home who was a pagan. The father of Timothy was a Greek, an unbeliever. He never attended worship with them. That's one reason Eunice surrounded Timothy with the best Christians that she knew.

Oh, the influence of Christian friends—especially mothers. Lord Byron said that he grew up to be a worthless man. He was born with a crooked foot. One time while in the way of his mother, she looked at him and said, "Get out of my way— you lame brat." He said that from hearing statements like that from his mother, day in and day out as he was growing up, he could not make himself to be what he knew he should be.

Mrs. Beecher, the mother of those two great preachers, Henry Ward and his younger brother, was asked, "How did your children become such great preachers and missionaries?"

She said, "I don't know. I really don't."

"But Mrs. Beecher, is there not some secret behind your spiritual success with your children?"

She said, "No, I just did what all mothers do every night before I went to bed, I bowed my knee on the floor and put my head on the bed and I said, 'Lord, let my boys be a preacher or a missionary for Jesus.' "

Did she just do what all mothers do? Oh, if that were only so. Do you want to rear a missionary? Mothers, bring them up like you know God would have you to do.

When Paul and Titus and some of the other brethren were in town on missionary work, do you know who invited them to dinner? Why it was Eunice. It was she who said, "Come over to our house—fellowship with us." Young Timothy was there playing around; he didn't look up to see somebody who was a bad influence on his life, he looked up into the face of the greatest missionary that ever lived—Paul. What an influence upon his life!

A man was admiring a beautiful tree in another yard and he said, "My, but that's a lovely tree. Why is there a crook in it?"

The owner said, "Well, when I planted that tree I had to go to New York and during my absence somebody leaned something heavy up beside it and it grew crooked. It has kept growing, but the crook is still there."

I am shocked and hurt to see how some Christian people allow their children to frequent certain places. Then when their children grow up crooked, the parents come to the pastor and ask, "Why is my child not loyal to the church?" Too often the correct answer is that the parents failed to provide the right discipline and the right associations.

Eunice knew the importance of Christian friends. It's important that your child know the greatest Christians you know. Don't hide them from your child. If he notices that mother and daddy never invite the best Christians they know but always the other kind of people to their home, the child is going to suspect that mother and daddy don't really want to be around good Christians. Wise parents will have great Christians in their home.

Help Him Love God's Work

How did Eunice do it? She really did it three ways. One way was by example. Do you think that Timothy was ever required to do anything that Eunice would not do? I doubt it. Eunice knew if she taught her child to do certain Christian things, she must do them herself. She must be an example. One of the great ways to teach your children how to be Christian is to be that yourself. Children usually have the habits that their parents have. If you have the habit of good Christian living, the likelihood is greater that your children will be deeply Christian.

Not only by example but also by teaching did Eunice help Timothy know of God's work. This is really where most of us fail. This is difficult for us to understand, but it's easier for us to live the Christian life than to teach it. It's usually the other way around. We usually can talk about it, but we can't live it. I have found just the opposite to be true among the best people that I know. They expect themselves to be at church when the doors open for this or that or the other, but it's all right for the young college student at home to sleep through Sunday School. It's all right to skip Church Training. After all, when you're a sophomore in college you don't care for that kid stuff any more. The greatest problem Christian parents have is not the living, but the teaching. If we live our Christianity but do not expect it of our children, we are saying to them, "I do it, but only because it's old-timey, only because it's habit, only because I'm expected to be there."

Teaching? Eunice taught. Have you ever heard, "as the twig is bent so shall the tree be"? There was an awful ruckus in a neighborhood in Scotland. A father was so upset that his boys had been involved that he ran out of the front door of his house, with one of those old blunderbuss guns, to get the ones who led his boys astray. In a cartoon portraying this particular incident, the man followed a path he suspected would lead him to the guilty. He followed the path through the woods and through the valleys and over the mountains and he came to a door, knocked on it, ready to shoot the one that opened it. It was a shock when his wife opened the door. The path had led right back to his own house.

Timothy was reared not only by example and teaching but also by experience. Timothy learned by experience. Eunice put him into the work. She wanted Timothy to love the work.

Now notice something, Paul "took and circumcised him because of the Jews which were in those quarters." Timothy was at a much older age than when a lad usually was circumcised. So for Timothy to be willing to do this at this age indicates the extent to which he would go to be qualified to belong to God's work.

Why did Paul have Timothy circumcised? His father was a Greek. Circumcision would help prove that Timothy meant business for God. It was an indication of religious cleanliness.

To what extent will you go to belong to God and have a clean, pure life, the kind of life that will let no man doubt your intentions and your sincerity. Do you want to rear a missionary? You can do it.

I'm going to rear a missionary and you are too. He'll either be a missionary for mediocrity, a missionary for half-hearted Christianity, a missionary to show a slothful father or mother, a missionary of sin, or a missionary for Christ, wherever he is or whatever he does. The question ought to be, what *kind* of missionary will I rear and will you rear?

Do you want to rear a missionary for Jesus? Help your child love the Book and know it. Help him to be a person who is associated with the best Christians you know. Help him to be in the thick of the work.

15

One Question at a Time

(Acts 16:5-15)

Our world is in need of people who are in the will of God. Our world needs spiritual giants. We need people of great Christian dimension.

Challenge yourself by saying: I've got to help the world. I've got to be a Gibraltar in the swirling oceans of life's indifferences. I've got to be a towering pinnacle over the other common forces of the world. I've got to stand on a rock foundation as others are sinking in the muck and mire of the sinful conditions of our day. I must be a spiritual giant myself. But how am I going to do it? How can I be in the center of God's will to shape my world for Christ?

The word of the Macedonian man, "Come over into Macedonia, and help us" (v. 9), may offer us some answers. In response, Paul asked some vital questions. If each of us will ask ourselves the same questions, we can better determine God's will, as Paul had to do in this situation. Let's look at these questions one at a time.

Where?

"Come over into Macedonia," the man in the vision said. "Come over . . . , and help us." Where? Macedonia, Paul, Macedonia. Macedonia belonged to Rome. Philippi, therein, belonged to Rome. It was a colony, which meant that Rome determined every governor, every official, every tax collector. It was a place where Rome had complete control. It was just a little bit of Rome set outside of Rome.

The history behind Macedonia and Philippi is interesting. Philippi was named for Philip of Macedonia, father of Alexander the Great. Philip also had a daughter whose name was Thesalo. Thessalonica was named for this daughter. What an interesting past this place has.

In Paul's vision came this voice, "Come over . . . , and help us." Many people think that Paul, in that vision, saw Alexander the Great speaking. Some think it significant, and I guess it is, that the theme of Alexander the Great's life was that he was going to marry the east to the west. He was going to conquer the world. And if there was ever a theme in the life of the apostle Paul, it was to have a wedding between the eastern and western worlds, to bring them together for Christ. Alexander the Great was a conqueror for the military cause of his day; Paul was a conqueror for the cross.

Others think, however, that the man in the vision was Luke, the author of the book of Acts and the Gospel. Well, in just a moment you'll discover, as we look more deeply into this passage, that the Holy Ghost kept his workers from some places. It could be that Paul interpreted his sickness, his thorn in the flesh, his weakened body due to the great amount of work that he had done, as the Holy Spirit telling him to go someplace else. Sometimes, God speaks through such circumstances. If so, Luke could have come to care for him, for Luke was a doctor. Luke could have been the Macedonian man who spoke to Paul, "Let us go into Macedonia." We don't know what man it was, but it is interesting to consider.

It is interesting to note that after the vision (v. 9), for the first time in this chapter, the plural word *we* appears in verse 10. "And after he had seen the vision, immediately we endeavoured to go into Macedonia."

We? Who is we? Paul had been by himself. By using the word *we*, Luke identifies himself as being with Paul—going to worship, going to serve, going to witness—Luke and Paul.

When seeking God's will, have you asked, Where? God, where do you want me—in the classroom? God, where do you want me—riding a tractor? Do you want me in industry with the roar of big machines? Is it there? Do you want me behind the wheel of a truck? God, do you want me in an airplane? God, do you want me on the battlefield? God, do you want me mending clothes and washing and ironing and sweeping and caring for a family? God, just where is it that you want me? If there is one essential question that you and I must ask ourselves when hearing the voice of God calling us, it is—where?

Paul, in doing the will of God, tried to go to Phrygia. God said no. He tried to go to Bithynia. God said no. Paul tried to go to Galatia. The Holy Spirit cut him off and said, "No, Paul, you cannot go." Were there not lost people in Bithynia? Were there not lost people in Galatia? Were there not lost people in Phrygia? Surely there must have been people who needed to hear about the Christian gospel. Paul must have reasoned like this to himself, but in discerning the will of God, What? is not the only question to be asked.

In the will of God, there is also a where. God does not only want us to do his will, but also he wants us to do his will where he wants us. The reason that Paul had to go to Macedonia was because that was where God wanted him to go. Now he might have had more converts down in Galatia. He might have had more converts in Bithynia, for the Bible does not record a great deal of success in Macedonia. So, God's *where* cannot always be based upon success or failure.

This story of Paul makes me think of Naaman. Naaman wanted to dip in the rivers of Abana and Pharpar the same amount of times that God's servant told him to dip in the river Jordan. Naaman learned he had to do not only what he was told but also where he was told to do it.

Let us be specific. Maybe within your own life there is a *where* that you have not asked. Maybe in my own life there is a *where* that I have not asked. Isn't there a part of my life and yours that is barricaded to God, a Macedonia that we have never touched? God looks down upon me and upon you and he says, "Oh, my Christian friend, come over into the Macedonia of selflessness and I'll loosen up your life." Then God looks at this part of my heart and says, "There is another Macedonia there. Come over into the Macedonia of concern for the lost and really serve there. Come over into the Macedonia of your heart that's marked out and bring people into loving fellowship."

Whatever it is that God is saying, he is saying you have a Macedonia. Some of you fathers may have a Macedonia of not leading your family spiritually, and God is saying to you, "Father, come over into this Macedonia and serve."

Paul's Macedonia was geographical and missionaries must interpret this geographically. Others, however, can not only interpret it geographically but can also interpret it personally. What is the Macedonia of your life and mine where God would call us to serve? Many of us have a Macedonia, and we know God would have us enter that Macedonia. Let's go over there and serve God where we have not been with him. Not only is there the question, Where? but there is also the very important question, When?

When?

Continue reading about the example of Paul. In verse 10, we read, "And after he had seen the vision, immediately we endeavoured to go into Macedonia." *Immediately! Immediately!* Do you know what I dislike about trying to correct my sins? It has to be done now. When Paul heard the voice of the Macedonian man, the Scripture says that he went "immediately." Oh, the difficulty that people find in doing the will of God *immediately.*

If there is a Macedonia you're leaving without attention, don't leave it any longer. Attend to it today. I've counseled with I don't know how many young couples throughout my twenty years of ministry. Oh, the things they've *planned* to do to place their homes upon the solid rock. I said to a man recently, "Friend, how long are you going to keep on like this?"

He said, "Preacher, I know I've got to straighten my life out. I know I've got to do better."

I said, "When?"

He said, "I don't know, I've—I've got to do it."

I said, "When?"

"Well, I'm going to do it."

I asked him, "Would you be willing to get on your knees right now and put your face upon this couch and pray to God that you'll never do that again?"

He answered me, "Now, preacher, I plan. . . ." I couldn't understand it—willing to go on with a practice in his marriage that was literally tearing it apart.

The thing that made David a giant killer was that he acted immediately. David came from the back of the line to the front of the line, burst out into the midst of the battlefield, picked up five stones, twirled his slingshot, embedded that little rock into the forehead of the big giant, who fell dead. Why? David acted immediately. Those others were talking about what they were going to do. But David got the job done. Most of us know the giant that we want to kill, but we're just too much of a coward to get out there on the field where it is hot and sweaty. The question is When? And the answer is, Immediately.

The boy left home a drunken sot. His mother prayed and prayed for him. Finally, after months and months, he cleaned up his life and came home just in time for his mother's funeral. He didn't know she had died. When they told him, he could not believe it and he said, "Turn back the clock, turn back the clock, I can't take it! It's not so. Turn the day back! I've got to see mother alive to let her know that I've changed."

That man leaned over his mother's casket and wept until his tears almost filled that box and he said, "Mother, Mother, Mother, I'm sorry." The problem was that he was sorry too late. What you plan to do isn't good enough. What you will do today is the only thing that matters.

How?

We must not just come immediately; *how* we come to Macedonia is important. We must come *trustingly*. If there is anything that is indicative of a life given to Christ, it is trust—it is faith. Don't you think for a moment that Paul enjoyed hearing about Macedonia. He had plans to go here and there and another place. But when God spoke, Paul was willing to go trusting, in faith; putting his confidence in God. Paul was willing to go, not knowing what was in Macedonia, not knowing if he would get stoned again as he did in Lystra, not knowing about the beasts of the forest, not knowing about the rulers. God spoke.

"When do I go, God?"

"You go immediately."

"How do I go, God?"

"You must go trustingly."

The only way that you and I will ever do the will of God is *trustingly*. God, what do you want me to do? Where do you want me to go? And when he speaks, you go in trust and you go in faith. Isaiah 12:2 says, "I will trust, and not be afraid."

You go not only trustingly but also *confidently*. You can find Paul saying, "I know," several times in the New Testament. Paul never doubted that he was in the will of God and that Jesus Christ was on his throne.

You can know what God wants you to do and you can know whether you are doing it. A person who is in God's will can know he is. And if you don't know, you're probably not in God's will. The will of God is that blessed assurance and that confidence of grace that lets you know that you've done the right thing. The man without commitment is also without confidence.

A soldier lay dying. A man rushed to his side and said, "What church are you?"

"I belong to the church of Jesus Christ," he said.

"No, I mean the denomination: I mean the persuasion."

The soldier, with dimming eyes and with a distraught look, gazed up into the face of the man and said, "Did you say persuasion? 'For I am persuaded, that neither death, nor life, nor angels, nor principalities, nor powers, nor things present, nor things to come, nor height, nor depth, nor any other creature, shall be able to separate us from the love of God, which is in Christ Jesus our Lord' " (Rom. 8:38-39).

Why?

You ask yourself, Where? You ask yourself, When? You ask yourself, How? Then you ask yourself, Why? In retrospect, almost, you have to ask yourself, Why? Don't you think that George Truett (for many years pastor of First Baptist Church, Dallas, Texas), when he was called as a little country boy, wondered why God called him? But when he stood before that great church, knowing thousands of people had been saved, that his church had supported many missionaries on foreign soil, and when he saw the working of God around the world because of him, he understood.

But you only ask one question at a time. You do not have the permission, you do not have the right to ask God, Why? until you have asked him Where? When? and How? But most people first ask God, Why? *Where? When? How?* and then *Why?*

Paul would have reasoned like this later on in his ministry. "Why did God call me to Macedonia? Well, don't you know about Philippi?" Paul would have asked. "Philippi was the church that wrote letters to me when I was feeling low. When I was poor they sent me money [and by the way, Philippi was the only church from which Paul received a financial grant. He refused it from Corinth, from Galatia, and from the other churches where he served]. Why did God call me to Macedonia? There is Philippi, what a present help in the time of need it has been to me."

I can think of another reason. It was Lydia. "Lydia? Paul, tell us about Lydia."

"Why, one day Luke and I went down to the riverside to preach because there was not a Jewish synagogue in Macedonia, and we met a very wealthy woman clad in clothes that made her stand out from the crowd. [Lydia was a woman who dyed clothing purple and the color purple had to be taken drop by drop from a rare species of a shellfish. The dealer had to be wealthy for one pound of wool dyed in this purple would cost over seventy-two dollars in our money today.] She was converted and went home and brought her family. They were converted, and I baptized them all. Do you know why the church at Philippi can give me money? Because Lydia gives money to the church at Philippi, and they send it on to me; therefore, I am able to go on and do the work that God wants me to do. You see, God had Lydia just waiting for the message, for he had a place for a person with financial means. He sent me there to be used of God." That would have answered Paul's why?

Pastor Louis Evans, for so long at the First Presbyterian Church in Hollywood, said that some years ago he attended a mission field in Africa. He visited with a doctor who gave up a very fine practice in order to be a missionary. The doctor said to him, "Mr. Evans, do you want to come in and see a major operation?"

Louis Evans said, "Yes, I do." So he went into the surgical theater but had to leave several times because of the heat

and the fumes. Finally, when the operation was all over, Mr.
Evans asked the missionary, "How many times a week do
you have to do this?"

He said, "Oh, usually several times a day."

"What would this operation have brought in the United
States? What would you have charged for this operation?"
The doctor told him five hundred dollars. "What do you get
out of it here?" Evans asked.

The doctor thought for a moment, beads of perspiration
all over his face and his lips purple with the tiresome effort
of this operation, and finally answered, "In my mind flashes
a little woman that had been brought to me screaming, 'Doctor, save my life!' " After a stare and a thought he answered,
"You know what I get? I get the gratitude of this dear woman
and the smile of my Master, and Doctor Evans, nothing could
make me richer." He knew *why* God used him.

There is a *where;* there is a *when;* there is a *how;* and if
you live it right, you'll see the *why.* It will be the most blessed
reward that you can have because you'll answer it this way—
"God used me, that's why."

16

A Song in the Night

(Acts 16:25-34)

"And at midnight Paul and Silas prayed, and sang praises unto God: and the prisoners heard them. And suddenly there was a great earthquake, so that the foundations of the prison were shaken: and immediately all the doors were opened, and everyone's bands were loosed. And the keeper of the prison awakening out of his sleep, and seeing the prison doors open, he drew out his sword, and would have killed himself, supposing that the prisoners had been fled. But Paul cried with a loud voice saying, Do thyself no harm: for we are all here. Then he called for a light, and sprang in, and came trembling, and fell down before Paul and Silas. And brought them out, and said, Sirs, what must I do to be saved? And they said, Believe on the Lord Jesus Christ and thou shalt be saved, and thy house. And they spake unto him the word of the Lord, and to all that were in his house. And he took them the same hour of the night, and washed their stripes: and was baptized, he and all his, straightway. And when he had brought them into his house, he set meat before them, and rejoiced, believing in God with all his house" (vv. 25-34).

A song in the night is certainly a great subject for us to think about at this time. How can one sing in the midst of the dark experiences of life?

A Song in the Night Must Come from a Seeing Heart

A song in the night must come from a seeing heart. When Paul and Silas were placed in the prison, they really didn't have anything there to remind them of their good home life. There wasn't anything about the meals that reminded them of the cooking they knew at home. There wasn't anything about the cruelty of those guards that reminded them of a mother's love, a father's care, or a relative's concern. And yet, they were able to believe with their heart instead of their eyes.

Some of us, who have great vision with our eyes, have blind hearts. Had I been in that prison, I probably would have thought to myself, What a miserable mess I'm in. What a horrible place to stay. Paul and Silas did not look through their eyes; they looked through their hearts. Both of these men had such a perception of God that in every moment of every day God was a living, dynamic, reality in their lives. Paul never had to call for God's presence, for to Paul, God was one that stayed in his life. For Paul to be absent from God was something that could not happen. Paul was so committed to the work of Jesus Christ that God was an integral part of his life.

Paul once said, "For me to live is Christ, and to die is gain" (Phil. 1:21). Paul said the only reason in the world that he lived was for the cause of Jesus. Since God is the giver of life, Paul felt it should be for God's sake. Paul had a heart that could see. He saw that in the midst of all of his difficulty, he was in the presence of God. Now God is perceived in two ways. God, first of all, is an objective God. That means that God exists; he is in heaven; he is living; he is moving; whether anybody believes it. That's God objectively. God is God.

He is also God subjectively. God is subjective in the sense

that you and I, to know and appreciate God, must know him subjectively from within. Many of us have the knowledge of God objectively. We believe that God is on his throne. He is in heaven. But this is not the only way that we must know God.

Believing in what some fainthearted souls call "a supreme being" is not good enough. We must not only know him objectively but also subjectively. That is, we must have had an experience with him that lives and stays close to us so that we don't doubt for a moment that God is remaining in the very portals of our heart. He has come personally and he is there to stay.

Paul knew God as few men know God but as all men are capable of knowing God. Paul knew God subjectively—from within. Paul, in prison, didn't see a prison. He looked around and saw God working out a plan in his life. Paul did not base his life upon circumstance. He based his life upon faith.

When a person wants a song in the night for life's darkest experiences, he must, as Paul, have a life that is governed not by the circumstances in which he finds himself, but by an attitude that is determined by the quality and the depth of his faith. Paul was seldom affected by his circumstances. Let the stripes come, let the shipwrecks be numerous, let the stones fall upon his skull at Lystra, let him be placed in a prison at Philippi, but you still see in the night of Paul's experience, one great anthem of praise unto God. Paul had faith within. If you only have faith without when the circumstances of sunshine change to the raging storms and life tumbles in upon you, you do not have a song to sing.

Do you want a song in the night? Do you want a song in your dark hour? Then you must be as Paul and have not only vision with your eyes but also vision with your heart and with your soul. Paul could sing a song in the night, for he could see with his heart. He saw God in prison with him. Isn't that a testimony of what God can do in the darkness of the night? "And at midnight," verse 25 says, "Paul and Silas prayed, and sang praises unto God."

Sometime ago I received a phone call about 5:30 in the morning. A voice on the telephone said, "Doctor Smith, will you come to the hospital, Mr. So and So has just died." She told me of a man with whom I had spent several hours, not only in his home but also at his bedside.

I hurriedly dressed and rushed down to the hospital, just in time to see the widow coming down the hospital steps. We met, embraced, and in the tenderness of the moment she said, "Oh, Doctor Smith, I've lost him. I've lost him." Then she looked up into my eyes, as if the whole atmosphere of the moment had changed, and said, "Do you know something—I thank God that he was Christian and I'll get to see him again."

For that lady, the moment was black, the moment was dark indeed, but in the midst of her anguish she could sing a song of praise unto God for she had a witness on the inside. She was able to see with her heart. In the deep pit of despair, she was able to sing a song unto God. You, too, can sing if God is within.

You can sing a song in the night if you have a seeing heart, if God is within. Read completely Romans 8:28: "All things work together for good to them that love God, to them who are the called according to his purpose."

A Song in the Night Will Bring the World to Its Knees

If there is any dynamic experience about this drama, it is the experience the jailer had with the Lord. Paul and Silas began to sing and praise God "and the prisoners heard them" (v. 25). They weren't singing like some of us sing today—with our teeth still together. They weren't afraid that somebody might hear that they had "A Blessed Assurance." They wanted to be heard.

The devil has chloroformed us into insensibility. The devil wants anything but joyful praise in the church. If the devil can get us so formal and so cold and so unrelated to the needs of the world, he'll win a great victory. He'll make us a museum of ecclesiastical art, and the world will go lost. But Paul and Silas were not like that. The devil's dope had not gotten to them, so they sang with all of their hearts.

Notice again, "the prisoners heard them." In fact, Paul and Silas sang so loud and joyfully, the world has heard their song of courage and faith as preachers have told this glorious story down through the centuries.

People complain about the tragedies in their lives, the discomforts, the heartaches (and we have them), but what a wonderful thing it is to see a Christian who has experienced the black night of sorrow and is able to say something good about God or to sing a song of praise about him. The world is listening not only to our singing but also to our lack of singing. It hears us when we say, "God shouldn't have done that to me." The world is listening. And we must realize that in the darkest times of our lives, we must be at our best as Christians. There must be singing instead of sighing. We must possess a singing soul instead of a sinking spirit.

Second Chronicles 28:27 tells about Hezekiah who came to the throne after a terrible reign of tragedy and godlessness by King Ahaz. Ahaz was a man that cared nothing about the statutes and laws of God. He led the people to paganism, to adultery, to every act of rebellion against the name of God. But when Hezekiah comes to the throne, "the burnt offering began, the song of the Lord began also with the trumpets" (2 Chron. 29:27). I like that, "the song of the Lord began also with the trumpets." The godly King Hezekiah brought the people back to God. They placed all of their earthly possessions upon the altar, giving up all they had. It seemed to be the darkest financial day in the life of Israel. The flames were shooting to the sky as they consumed the accumulated possessions of the Israelites. As the heat from those destroying flames warmed their faces, they sang a song of the Lord with trumpets.

If we have a song in the night, some of the world will bow its knees before us. The jailer saw that Paul and Silas were men of faith. He saw the other prisoners run and the other jailers as they went fleeing for their lives. He might have said to himself, Look at me. I had my sword at my heart ready to fall upon it because I was scared that I would get the same punishment as these men were to get because I let them loose.

When he looked at Paul and Silas he saw that their eyes were steady. He saw that they were standing straight. He saw that they were standing alert, with confidence that this ordeal was going to work out. He realized that he was no longer the captor but captive of what they had to offer. They were so serene. They were so sedate. They were so calm. So impressed he became with their calm confidence in the throes of tragedy, he said with a searching heart, "What must I do to be saved?"

The world might be asking you and me that more often if they saw us say to God in our dark moments, "God, I still love you in spite of all of this." Then the world might say, "My, if that's what knowing Jesus means, then I want some of that."

If you sing a song in the night, you'll find somebody in the world bowing their knee to Jesus because they saw Jesus standing erect in you.

A Song in the Night Shall
Open Doors to Freedom

There is a great captivity in our land today. It is the captivity of persons who have never had a song in the night in life's experiences. They are so captive that they live in a world all by themselves. They are in prison indeed. Well, Paul and Silas began to sing in the night and the earthquake came. It shook the prison foundation, all the doors were opened, and the prisoners could have gone free. What an experience it was!

It's no different today for you and me in the loss of a loved one or in a deep tragedy of life that we are able, by God's grace, to sing a song. We find the air is fresher, the birds sing a little sweeter, that all is different. We shall discover something that we have never known before—and that is a freedom that only comes to those who are able to praise God in life's more difficult experiences. If we sing in the night, God's never-before-seen power comes to our aid.

I read an amusing story about some men who lived years ago in England. Three preachers came into a town. They preached and one of them was put in jail. The second one preached and he was put in jail. The third one preached and he was put in jail. Well, it wasn't long until all three of them, in the same cell, were singing praises unto God. People were disturbed because three preachers were singing and upsetting everybody. So the magistrate said, "Separate these men; they are disturbing us more now than when they were preaching."

So they separated the men, leaving one by himself, putting one in the cell with a robber, and the other in a cell with another criminal. Well, it was not long until the preacher who was put into the cell with the robber had converted the robber and both of them were singing. The preacher who was put in the cell with the other criminal converted him— then both of them were singing. Instead of three preachers singing, five Christians were singing.

The magistrate said to the guard, "I thought I told you to separate them."

He said, "I did."

The magistrate said, "Separate them again."

The guard said, "If I do, the whole jail will catch this thing. You'd better leave them alone."

What a testimony this is to the power of Christ. In the midst of a prison, revival broke out.

Sing a song in the night and freedom will come—freedom that you've never known before. Do you think Paul was really captive before the earthquake? Paul was as free before the earthquake as he was after. His freedom was not based upon what was on the outside; his freedom was based on what was on the inside. And in this case it was true that "stone walls do not a prison make or iron bars a jail." Paul had been set free within his heart.

A minister told of a lady who had had a terrible tragedy in her life. She was looking around in despair and feeling sorry for herself. She said to a wise Christian, "You know, I wish that God had never made me."

In reply the Christian lady said something that all of us need to remember, "My dear, God has not made you yet. He's in the process of making you, and you must be patient while the Maker molds you into what he wants you to be."

17
Saved—What Must I Do?

(Acts 16:32-40)

When the Philippian jailer saw his danger, he asked this most important question, "What must I do to be saved?" That question surely has been used by every evangelistic preacher in some revival. It is, of course, the most critical question of life.

But, "Saved, what must I do?" is also a vital question. Too often we forget that being saved is the beginning of the Christian life, not the end. After we have been saved, there are some things we must do. I think the jailer is a good example of what a person's salvation should make him be and do.

He Wanted His Life to Show That He Had Been Saved

Notice that the jailer was baptized. When the jailer was saved, born again, and experienced the cleansing power of Jesus Christ in his life, Paul told him that it was a command of the Lord and a witness to the saints for him to be baptized. Paul told him it was a practice of the New Testament church. He said, in essence, "Well, if that's what I'm supposed to do, then I'm going to do it."

Now I would not venture to say that every man who has been saved has been baptized, but I would venture to say this: I honestly believe, according to God's Word, that a man who has been born again, a man who has become a Christian, a man who has been saved will do everything possible to let the world know that he has been saved. The Christian wants the world to know that Christ has made a big difference in his life. Therefore, if a man, who has been saved, is told that one of the things he needs to do to indicate his salvation is to be baptized, he should be eager to do it. It is difficult to believe that a man who has been saved will refuse to be baptized.

I do not agree with our friends who say that baptism is absolutely necessary for salvation. I believe that it is an absolute necessity for a man, who has been saved, to indicate every way he can his commitment to Jesus Christ. One of the finest, noblest, worthwhile indications is a person's willingness to be buried in the baptismal waters with Jesus. I just cannot believe that a person could be saved and refuse to be baptized. For if God could save a person and not change him enough to want to represent his death and burial and his resurrection, that person would have had a very anemic experience. A man who has been saved will want to do everything in his power to let the world know what he has done.

I imagine that Paul told the jailer, "Now what you need to do is to be baptized and go to church." The Philippian jailer might have said to Paul, "What else, what else, what else? What else can I do? Is that all? Is there a large button that I can wear on my lapel? Is there a sign that I can hold in my hand that says, Guess what? The old, rough Philippian guard, who stood over that jail and represented evil, now has been converted to the cause of that carpenter of Nazareth and he walks today with a difference.'"

What a contrast that is to what is often said or implied today. "I'm saved, I've escaped hell, now I'll forget about it." Every Christian should ask himself, Now that I'm saved, how can I indicate to everyone that I belong to God?

A man said to me sometime ago, "I'm a better Christian than most church members." I wanted to say to him, I don't believe you. He may have been as good as some of our church members, but he was also as bad as some of them. I told him that at least the church members were in the place that could help them be better and do better. We all agree that a church is not a museum for saints; it is a hospital for sinners. I just cannot believe, all things being equal, that two men are the same spiritually if one of them says he is a Christian but has refused to join a church. Neither do I believe that the Bible says that a man who says he is saved but is faithless in the church has ever had a genuine experience with Christ.

Would you believe a man to be a Marine if he refused to join the corps or a Mason who refused to join the lodge? God's Word says that when a man is born again there is a difference. If a man has not had a definite change in his life, he has not ever known the Christ that the New Testament men knew. If Christ is too weak to make a change in a man's life, he is too weak to form the earth, to place the sun in its orbit, or to take the stars and to fling them into the skies. God is what changes a man; if there has been no change, there has been no conversion.

The laws of the land tell us that a man can be married to a woman simply by going to a preacher or justice of peace, and if the license is in order, they are married. That's a law of the land—they are legally married. But you and I know there are some marriages that have taken place, legally, but they have never been spiritual marriages in the eyes of God. There is a difference, a vast difference between a legal marriage and a good marriage.

There's also a spiritual law that when a man accepts Jesus Christ as Savior and Lord, he is born again, he is saved. That's a spiritual law. It's the law of God's Book. Some Christians are just legally married to Christ and no more. They will make heaven, but barely, and the journey there will not have the thrill and joy it should. It does make you question a person's salvation when they refuse to do what God says to do.

Jesus went so far as to say, "If ye love me, keep my commandments" (John 14:15). Some people live in disobedience

on one hand and on the other hand say they love the Lord.
Jesus said these are incompatible. He said love and obedience
go together. Yet, all over our world, there are people who
say they have been born again, but there is not one indication
of it. A man who has been born again, the Scriptures indicate,
will be obedient to what Christ has told him to do.

You Must Indicate Some Christian Love and Concern

This old guard probably mistreated Paul and Silas, pushing
them into jail and cursing them all the way. Then all of that
was changed. He experienced salvation. Something new came
over this man's life.

After his conversion, the Bible says that he took Paul and
Silas to his house and placed water on their stripes, cleaned
them, and put meat before them—not just black-eyed peas
and corn bread, but meat. This man had been changed. He
gave the best that he had to these men who were once a
threat to his own security. All of a sudden he was different.
Could a psychologist have done that? Could a psychiatrist have
accomplished that change? Could all of the effort of the sociol-
ogist do that? No, but Jesus could; when Jesus Christ comes
into a man's life, he is changed from the bottom of his feet
to the top of his head.

The Christian is concerned. What a wonderful thing it is!
There is a love and a closeness about people who are saved,
that are just not known by any other people in the world.
People who have been born again, whether they are white
and rich, black and poor, or yellow and foreign, when they
come to meet on the common soil of Golgotha's skull, are
one in Christ. There's a love and concern and a care, when
you've been born again, that comes by the indwelling presence of the Holy Spirit.

A former Hindu and a New Zealander met on a ship; they
could not speak one another's language. They could not tell
each other that they had been born again, but each of them

did know Christ. Finally, they noticed one another's Bible which became a point of communication. They began to point to each other's Bible, but they still could not communicate in language. Finally, one of them said, "Hallelujah." The former Hindu man said, with a great smile on his face, "Hallelujah." The other one said, "Amen." The former Hindu said, "Amen." These words that could not be translated into their own language, became their source of communicating their Christian commitment. So everytime they met from that time on, it was "hallelujah" and "amen."

Every Christian should love his Christian brethren in a special way because we all have been washed by the same atoning blood of Calvary's cross. We ought to love our brethren wherever they are, whatever they look like, whatever their responsibility in life.

You Must Be Happy

You must rejoice. You must have an enthusiastic life for Christ. I just doubt if there is a drab Christian on the face of the earth. I've seen some drab church members, but I doubt if I've ever seen a drab Christian. The Philippian jailer had been saved, and he was rejoicing. He knew what it was to be changed by Christ. The Scripture says, "and he . . . was baptized, he and all his, straightway. And when he had brought them into his house, he set meat before them and rejoiced" (vv. 33-34).

What did Paul tell that lovely church at Philippi? "Rejoice in the Lord alway: and again I say, Rejoice" (Phil. 4:4). What do we have to rejoice about? We have the same things to rejoice about that the Philippian jailer had to rejoice about. What are those things? One thing is that *fear is gone.* The jailer was facing imminent danger. When he saw the blackness of the sky and the earthquake splitting the ground, he came running to Paul and Silas and asked them, "What must I do to be saved? Anything, what must I do?" Now, he wasn't asking

what must I do to be saved from the magistrate for Paul and
Silas had told him that all of the prisoners were intact. If he
had been asking that, he would not have asked Paul and Barnabas for they could not have helped him with the magistrate—
the magistrate was their enemy. He was asking a theological
question, for he had probably heard Paul and Silas preach
throughout the community before they were ever jailed. He
had heard them talk about being saved, being converted, following Jesus. He said, "What must I do to be saved?"

If there is any need in our world today, it is to let the lost
man know that he is in danger of hell fire if he does not
accept Jesus Christ. It's not a cruel thing. Do you know that
the word *hell* came more from the lips of Jesus than the word
heaven ever did? In fact, twice as much. Jesus wanted to warn
men who were outside of his will and his purpose that there
was a danger, there was a hell. If a man didn't accept him,
he was going to spend eternity in a devil's hell. The Philippian
jailer knew that and when he accepted Jesus Christ, he rejoiced for he knew that there was no longer a chance of hell,
no longer a problem of eternal death. We ought to rejoice.

This man also rejoiced over his *inner peace*. He had never
known such peaceful tranquility. He had worried about all
the affairs of life, but all of a sudden the burden was gone.
The weight was lifted from his back.

In the old days when castles were built, aqueducts were
built to carry water from the outside into the castle. Enemies
discovered that if they stopped the water, the people die of
thirst; they could defeat them. Later on in history, castles
were built over sparkling streams. When the enemy would
come from the outside, the water supply would still be fresh,
sparkling, clear, and clean because it sprang up from the inside
where the enemy couldn't get to it.

That's what a Christian is—a life over the stream. No matter
what the outside world thinks, no matter what the opposition
does, perennially in the heart of the Christian there is a spar-

kling artesian well from which he can drink. What a blessing it is to have that refreshing water from within from which we can continually and eternally draw. That is another reason the jailer rejoiced.

He rejoiced out of anticipation for better days. One reason for the lack of joy in Christian lives is the lack of vision and anticipation. All through the Bible, there are remarks of anticipation of joy. Psalm 126 is a most important chapter:

When the Lord turned again the captivity of Zion, we were like them that dream. Then was our mouth filled with laughter, and our tongue with singing: then said they among the heathen, The Lord hath done great things for them. The Lord hath done great things for us; whereof we are glad. Turn again our captivity, O Lord, as the streams in the south. They that sow in tears shall reap in joy. He that goeth forth and weepeth, bearing precious seed, shall doubtless come again with rejoicing, bringing his sheaves with him.

Then in Isaiah 12:3, "Therefore with joy shall you draw water out of the wells of salvation." Isaiah 61:10, "I will greatly rejoice in the Lord, my soul shall be joyful in my God; for he has clothed me with garments of salvation, he hath covered me with the robe of righteousness, [notice this anticipation] as a bridegroom decketh himself with ornaments, and as a bride adorneth herself with her jewels."

Time and again the Bible records the rejoicing of the early saints was over anticipation of what was to come.

For every despairing note you can offer, the Bible can offer a thousand words that say, "Rejoice, rejoice." You and I think the Christian life has been wonderful, but it hasn't been anything compared to what God has in store for all of us in heaven some day. If you get worried, fretful, or discouraged, just begin to anticipate what is yet to come to those that know the Lord.

18

Life's Unsoiled Dimensions

(Acts 17:15-21)

Occasionally people will ask, quite dejectedly, Is there something in life that *is* what it is made out to be? People of all ages are asking such questions today, for they sense the impurity and dirtiness of this world. They really want to know what is real and genuine and honest and pure in this world. They are getting tired of the thin facade of the world's insincerities. The memory of national and international political intrigue is still with us. We have had reasons to wonder about and be skeptical of some of the affairs of life.

Yet the picture is not all dark. The apostle Paul, in preaching to the cultured people of Athens, pointed them to dimensions that have never been soiled by dishonesty, fraud, deception, and superficial motives. Acts 17:15-21, records Paul's description of some of the unsoiled dimensions in life. Here a Christian can see every reason to shout and every sinner can see a clear vision of hope. These dimensions give a zest to life that only the Christian can fully realize. I want you to notice these unsoiled dimensions of life.

There Is an Unsoiled Person

Paul could have preached a number of things to the Athenians. Certainly he could have started off preaching a sermon on philosophy, for no group of people in all of the world loved to philosophize quite like the Athenians. Paul could have preached a sermon on political theory, for those people were politically inclined. Paul could have preached a sermon on moral consciousness, for no group of people needed a sermon on moral consciousness quite like the Grecian people. He could have preached a sermon on righteousness, on goodness, on religious doctrine and dogma, but he did not.

Paul preached great truth to these cultural people—people known for their intelligence and scholastic achievement. He did not come with anything scholastic. He did not preach anything academic. He did not preach some intellectual jargon that would impress them, but he offered them a person who is unsoiled in life's dimensions. He came with Jesus. Verse 18 says, "he preached unto them Jesus." In life's dimensions the only person who is unsoiled by the hatred and discords of man and the imperfections of humanity is Jesus Christ.

Paul looked at those people disgruntled with Caesar. They couldn't care less about the Stoic. They were having trouble with the philosopher who sat there on the curb stones looking up into heaven speculating about truth. They had problems galore with the personalities of their day, and so Paul came with one personality with which no man can honestly find fault. The only unsoiled person in life's dimensions is Jesus Christ.

Our world is unhappy with personalities. In Europe some men who used to stand tall are being ejected from their thrones. The Shah of Iran toppled. Men who once were great leaders are now being ridiculed by people who once voted for them. A president of the United States is forced to resign. In South America, when you can pick up your newspaper and read about South American countries, almost every day a top man has been voted out, assassinated, or exiled to a faraway island. People are disgruntled with personalities; for within them all, they find imperfection. They find something they do not like.

Look closely at Jesus Christ, a man who never wrote a book, a man who never went very far from his home, a man who had never attended college; yet, this man, who does not have many of the accomplishments of a man today, affected the life of men upon earth as no other man has ever affected the thinking of man. He was sinless—perfect.

What I am saying is that Jesus Christ is the only unsoiled person in life's dimensions. Go to great men, go to great leaders, go to men of unusual accomplishments; inevitably you will come away disappointed. In them all there are imperfections. In Christ there is no sin. In him there is no guile. In him there is no fault. Jesus was never jealous. Jesus never hated anyone. Jesus never had to ask for forgiveness of his sins because he never had anything he needed forgiven.

He is the perfect Son of God. Mussolini and Hitler and Napoleon used to talk about what they were, what they were going to do, and the people would laugh. But Jesus came and he spoke with authority and said, "Verily." He didn't use the adverbs we use. He didn't use words like *usually*. He said, "Verily, I say unto you." And even the enemy said of him, "Never man spake like this man" (John 7:46).

The world today is coming to the drug counters across our land for medicine for the body and to churches for medicine for the soul. Many times the people are disappointed; for even in many of the churches of Jesus Christ today, men are giving everything else but Jesus, and there is no cure for the ills of the world except through him.

Oh, how pitiful is the church congregation that has to listen to one social sermon after another, when if the preacher would lift up Jesus and bring the people to the cross and have them look into the face of the man of Nazareth, then they would be so richly blessed. I agree with the statement, "When you look at Jesus, nothing else ever satisfies again." Joseph Sizoo said about our Lord, "You might as well try to untwist the moonbeams that shine down on the hills around you, as to try to untwist the memory of Jesus Christ from the heart and the hope of mankind for you cannot do it." And then he adds,

"The world is not through with Jesus Christ, but it is through without him." I agree.

The unsoiled person in life's dimensions is Jesus Christ. Why even the people of his day knew Jesus' perfection. When he walked into the presence of Peter, Peter said unto him, "Depart from me for I am a sinful man, O Lord" (Luke 5:8). The thief on the cross said about himself and the other thief, "We indeed justly; . . ." and then he gestured to Jesus and he said, "but this man has done nothing amiss." Procula looked over at her husband, Pilate, and said to him, "Have nothing to do with this just man" (Matt. 27:19).

Richard Guilder said about our Lord:

> If Jesus Christ is man,
> And only man I'll say,
> Of all mankind, I will follow him
> And follow Him all the way.
> If Jesus Christ is God,
> The only God I'll swear,
> I'll follow Him through heaven and hell
> Through sea and sky and air.

There Is an Unsoiled Place

Verse 18 says, "And he [Paul] preached unto them Jesus and the resurrection." The resurrection was a miraculous event. The Athenians knew how to sit and speculate, but Jesus never had to do any of that, for Jesus never sought for the truth. He was the Truth. Jesus never did try to find God, for he was God. Jesus never did try to find light for he was the Light. Jesus never tried to find any nourishment from great truth, for he said, "I am the Bread of life" (John 6:35,48). When Jesus' spiritual tongue was parched, he didn't ask for some great philosopher who lived before he was born. He said, "I am the water of life" (Rev. 21:6).

Paul may have asked, "Do you know what the resurrection

means? It means that Jesus conquered death and the grave and he ascended unto the Father and he is there preparing a place for you and me." Paul knew about the resurrected Lord. One day when Paul was on the way to Damascus, Jesus Christ came in a shining light and Paul, being blinded, fell upon his knees and was miraculously and gloriously converted. The resurrection was a personal event to Paul. But it meant something more than just that to him. It meant that Christianity was fresh, alive, and radiant. So he talked about the resurrection because he knew that the resurrection meant that there was a place prepared for the saved.

The Athenians had known war; they had known cruelty; they had known murdering; they had known drunkenness; they had known immorality as only few people had known it, even with all their culture and art. Paul was saying to the Athenians, "There is an unsoiled place to which you can go."

Dr. Dale of Birmingham said one time he was preparing an Easter sermon on the resurrection and he got to thinking about it. "Christ, alive, imagine that. Jesus alive." He got up from his desk, put his pen down, and he began to ponder over and over again, "Jesus is alive." He began to shout it, "Jesus is alive, imagine that. Christ is alive. One day I will be with him. Heaven, heaven, what a wonderful place it will be!"

There is an unsoiled place. When you are troubled and discouraged, think about it. You will find a new dimension to life, as you keep before you the unsoiled place in life's dimensions.

There Is an Unsoiled Peace

The people of Athens did not know peace. They did not know a person who was unsoiled, a place that was unsoiled, and they certainly knew nothing about an unsoiled peace. Paul was so discouraged because he said, here in the book of Acts, how disappointed he was that they were worshiping one idol after another. They had their statues and worshiped them. They had their stones, their buildings, their cathedrals, and they worshiped them. But their peace was soiled by shallow worship.

We don't fall and worship a stack of rocks, but my, we are an idolatrous people. The world is seeking after pleasure. Man has more leisure time. We are making an idol of pleasure.

We're making an idol of sex. A preacher told me sometime ago about a group of young men from California who came into his small city with an expressed goal to rob every young girl in that city of her purity, of her virginity, of all that was wholesome. In far too many cases (one case would be too many), they reportedly succeeded.

Look up to Christ and find the peace and the harmony and the happiness that comes from him, instead of making an idol of fruitless pleasure that drags a man down.

We have also made a god of financial gain. Oh, the people working madly sunup to sundown, sacrificing their family upon the altar of warped ideals. They say, "I must have more, a bigger car, a bigger home, a bigger bank account." God's spiritual values are forgotten.

Another false god of our day is our idolatry of apathy. Can you worship apathy and complacency? I think you can. People are proud today, and they are worshiping the fact that nothing upsets them anymore. They no longer care that the preacher is unable to preach good enough and hard enough to make them shed tears over the world conditions. They are worshiping their coldness. God is looking down upon them, as he looked at Athens, and is disturbed that they are going after idols. Some people are no longer disturbed that they cannot be disturbed and that, indeed, is disturbing in itself.

What is your false god? Look at what these people were—Epicureans and Stoics. The Epicureans lived for pleasure. They believed in some god, but they believed that he was unrelated to the world. They believed that everything that brought man pleasure was all right. Epicureans, with that stupid and godless philosophy, are with us today.

The Stoics believed that every once and awhile the world would end and start all over again. They believed that nothing mattered. Therefore, don't care about anything, don't be upset, don't be disturbed, for everything that will be will be was their idea.

But the Stoics were wrong, as were the Epicureans. We can bring the world an unsoiled person. We can tell them about an unsoiled place. We can give them the unsoiled peace of Jesus Christ that is not affected if the world tumbles. It is only affected by the life and Spirit of Jesus Christ—and within that Spirit and life only can be found life's unsoiled dimensions.

19

No Time to Be Afraid

(Acts 18:4-11)

We must never fear the responsibility we have as Christians. With courage and determination, we must take up the torch of Christian commitment. We must not be afraid because, even though there will be forces to oppose us, the victory is assured. When you really mean business for God, there are apparent reasons to be afraid; but the fear fades when you see that the apparent is not always real.

There is no shortage of fear today. People are afraid of the future. They are afraid of the past, with its haunting memories that come marching into their present with spike shoes. They are certainly worried about the present because the possibilities of failure and discomfort and insecurity seem ever so real. People in our world are afraid.

The body of a young hippie girl was found sometime ago in Los Angeles thrown over a stripped umbrella rod. The jagged rod pierced her body, these words of Carlyle, that she had scribbled with a felt pen on the back of her sweatshirt, could be read. "What is life? It is nothing but a thawing iceberg on a sea with a sunny shore. Gay we sail, it melts beneath us, we are sunk and sing no more."

What do you think God would say to us about this matter of being afraid? Paul met discouragement, and God saw his ghastly gloom and said something like this to him, "Paul, this is no time to be afraid" (see Acts 18:4-11). Let's look more closely at this dramatic truth.

165

Discouragement for the Christian Is Only Temporary

Paul was very discouraged. The Jews turned their backs on him and said, "Paul, we don't want anything to do with you."

Paul said, "If that's how you feel, then I don't want anything to do with you. I've tried and I've tried and I've tried. Let your own blood be upon your own heads." He turned his back upon the Jews; from that day forward, the very emphasis of his preaching and ministry was to the Gentile people.

He was discouraged. The Bible uses the phrase, "Paul was pressed in the spirit" (v. 5). We would say he was depressed, discouraged, or despondent. God came to Paul and said, "Be not afraid, but speak, and hold not thy peace." Paul was discouraged, but he knew that our Christian discouragement is always temporary. A Christian knows that he has victory on the inside. He has won the battle. His salvation is secure. The greatest moments of his life are still awaiting him; no matter what comes, he has an artesian well bubbling up on the inside. Discouragement and despondency and failure can't last. For the Christian, discouragement at its worst is only temporary. The Christian works *from* victory not *to* victory. Our victory was won at Calvary. The Christian knows that if he has a bad day, there's a week of goodness ahead. If he has a bad week, there's a month of joy ahead. If he has a terrible month of despondency, there is a year for which he must rejoice in his future.

Look at Paul. The greatest travels that he ever made were after this incident. The greatest letters that he ever wrote were after this. The greatest words that he ever spoke, he spoke after the time of his black hour of discouragement.

I read where the devil was going out of business (I wish that were so, but it is not), so he sold all of his tools. He had a lot of tools. He had hatred, malice, jealousy, pride, haughtiness, and backbiting. All of those tools were for sale. But then he had one that was priced a hundred times above all of his other tools of destruction, and that tool was the tool of discouragement. Somebody asked, "Mr. Satan, why is this tool more costly than the others?"

And Satan said, "The tool of discouragement has done more to defeat the work of God than any other tool that I've ever used. That's why it will cost you more to take it from me."

I have a picture of my father standing on top of some lumber that had been blown down. The lumber happened to be a church that he was constructing. Much of the church building was up, but a little whirlwind that didn't touch anything else came through that little community in Dallas and blew the church down. What a tragedy. It was especially horrible for me because my dad put a big nail keg out there and said, "Bailey, take this hammer and take all of the sixteen penny nails out of those two by six's and put them in the keg. When the keg is full, you can go into the house." That keg looked to me as big as one of these great water towers you see in large cities, but finally I filled it.

What a discouraging thing it was for my family and our church. There was not one penny of insurance, at that point, on the building. What did my dad do? He led the church to start over. Today a beautiful building is there where the blessed gospel of Christ is preached.

Somebody Will Always Be Interested in What You're Saying About Christ

There is no time to be afraid because as long as there is air to breathe, water to drink, earth upon which to walk, there will be somebody in this world who will listen to what you have to say about Jesus. As long as there are people on the earth, there will be people who want to hear the gospel. God said to Paul, "I have much people in this city [Corinth]" (v. 10). Now what did he mean when he said this to Paul? I think he meant, "Paul, you're looking at the corruption in Corinth, you're looking at all that is discouraging." Historically that would not have been hard to see corruption because Corinth, even though it had a church, was greatly characterized by its sins and decadence. God meant that there were many people in Corinth who, if they heard the message of Christ, would be sympathetic to it. They would give a listening ear.

Isn't that encouraging to you? Don't be afraid when people don't listen. Some people will always listen because God has many people on this earth who will always be receptive. Paul understood two things for sure. He knew that a Christian must always speak whether anybody listens. And he knew, second of all, that somebody will always be willing to respond to the gospel. God said, "Paul, don't get out of business, just start giving the business to somebody else, just start witnessing in another place." Paul then began to preach to the Gentiles. Keep on preaching because somebody will always listen.

God said, "My word shall never return unto me void" (Isa. 55:11). Do you know there is no way to waste a gospel sermon? Do you know there is no such thing as an unsuccessful witness? Do you know that there is no such thing as a failure in telling people about Jesus, for if they don't respond immediately, somebody will later. Do not be afraid when somebody will not listen—somebody else will. Just keep speaking. Do not be afraid, "hold not thy peace," keep on telling.

We Have an Untiring Partner

Look at verse 10, "For I am with thee, and no man shall set on thee to hurt thee." Look at the word "for." What does it mean, "For"? It means "because." What was the Lord saying? "Paul, if you had no other reason in the world to be bold and speak out, just because I'm with you is enough."

Look at the next words, "I am with thee." Who is he talking about? The One who took the stars and flung them into space to lighten a darkened sky. He made the universe like he wanted it. He made man and woman in his own image. He is the One called Omnipotent—all powerful; Omniscient—all knowing; Omnipresent—every place present. This God, this ruler of the heavens, this One majestically sitting on his throne will be with you.

That's the same kind of truth that Daniel knew in the lion's den. That's the kind of truth that let Moses courageously lead the children of Israel to the border of Canaan. That's the very type of truth that took Elijah to the top of Mount Carmel. That's the same kind of God that led Bill Wallace to China where he died.

If you don't know God's presence, then you have a need today that only God can supply. There is no time to be afraid because if there is discouragement, it's only temporary. There is no time to be afraid because if someone shuts the door in your face, someone else will listen. There is no time to be afraid when one is believing the great promises, presence, and power of our mighty God.

20
The Trouble with Trouble

(Acts 18:12-18)

Every preacher has in his files of sermons many messages around the theme of overcoming difficulties. Such titles in my files are "Failure Need Not Be Final," "Detained But Not Defeated," "Victory in Defeat," "Triumph in Tragedy," indicating that trouble can successfully be coped with.

The theme is a good one because man must be able to face his problems with courage. He must be bold in his circumstances. He is capable of overcoming his difficulties. Surely a circumstance of great disadvantage can be turned into something victorious and accomplishing.

Where is it in trouble that we really find ourselves in danger? Where is it in the midst of trouble and where is it in the midst of difficulty that we really find our weak spots? Where do we find ourselves ready to fall, ready to trip? What is it about trouble that really makes us incapable of carrying on? What is it that we must watch when trouble comes? It is true that in life we can turn the pitiful into the pleasant. We can turn the upset into the uplift, and we can turn the hard blow into the wonderful blessing.

That's why I have entitled this chapter, "The Trouble with Trouble." What is it in trouble that really gives us trouble? If a man can overcome his trouble and his difficulty with just a little bit of faith in God, then what is it in trouble that gives him the greatest trouble? Acts 18:12-18, offers us some answers.

Trouble May Cause Us to Compromise Our Convictions

Paul was in trouble with the Jews and with the officials of his day because he had convictions. Paul believed in his convictions with all of his heart. Because of this Paul got into trouble.

The Jews might have reasoned, Paul has taught contrary to the Jewish law and he is persuading some men that this is the way to be. And so they said to him, "Now, Paul, this isn't the way that it ought to be." They placed Paul before the chief leader, Gallio. Gallio cared nothing about all of this because he felt it was a Jewish matter.

Paul was in a great deal of difficulty, and we find in verse 14 that Paul tried to speak but he could not. "And when Paul was now about to open his mouth, Gallio said unto the Jews . . . ." I think Paul was going to make a reaffirmation of the truth that he had spoken. Paul knew that when trouble comes because of a conviction, people have a tendency to compromise that conviction in order to escape the trouble they are in.

We have heard the phrase "peace at any price." Some people have this type of philosophical attitude as Christians, "Just so long as I don't have any enemies; just so long as my life is 100 percent compatible; just as long as I don't get into any trouble with my friends or people in the city; just so long as I keep social face—that's all that matters. So I'll compromise. I'll give in. I'll retreat."

When a person finds himself in trouble, there is definitely a tendency to compromise. That is one of the troubles with trouble. The trouble with trouble is that you and I often find ourselves wanting to get out of trouble so badly that we are willing to give up something that's more important than life itself—simply for a moment of peace and satisfaction and fleshly contentment.

How many of us have found ourselves at the crossroads of

compromise? We have discovered sometimes that if we go
the way of the world, there can be no trouble for us. But if
we go the way of the Bible (at least if we go the way of the
Bible fully), somebody is not going to like it, so we turn our
backs upon the Bible and decide to take the road that leads
the way the world wants to go. There are not as many restric-
tions on the broad road—the road that leads to destruction.
That's the trouble with trouble.

Notice how Paul got into this trouble. Paul tried to open
his mouth and he couldn't speak, but they said "this fellow
persuadeth men to worship God contrary to the law" (v. 13).
Paul was preaching that the only way a person can be saved
is through the death of Jesus Christ on the cross. The Jews
didn't believe that. The Jews believed it was by keeping the
law. Therefore, Paul got into trouble.

Paul faced a crossroad. Do you know what Paul could have
said? He could have said, "Well, now, I need to compromise
a little bit and get out of this trouble." Paul could have rational-
ized and said, "Now there's no use to my sticking to my guns
on this because I can be down the road in just a moment
preaching to somebody else." But Paul wasn't willing to compromise his convictions because he knew that people have
a tendency, in order to get out of trouble, to compromise.

William Temple was a great preacher of another day. He
said that the age in which he lived was characterized by the
life of a man who came to a shop window and took all of
the expensive merchandise tags and put them on the cheap
articles and took the articles that were expensive and put
cheap price tags on them. And, therefore, when people came
in to buy they paid a great price for that which was cheap
and a cheap price for that which was valuable. William Temple
said to his congregation that that's the way our life is today.

The trouble with trouble is that it has a tendency to make
us want to compromise our convictions. Paul could have said,
"All right, men, I changed my mind. I'm not willing to pay

the price. Let me out, I don't want anything to do with this."

This reminds me of the two little boys who were looking at their grandfather's sword. One little boy said, "Everytime I look at Grandfather's sword, it makes me want to go to war."

The other little boy said, "Yes, and everytime I see his wooden leg, it makes me want to stay at home." Sometimes we are not willing to pay the price that it takes to keep the convictions that God would have us to have.

Trouble Sometimes Comes from Unexpected Sources

In this passage, we're not too impressed with the fact that the Jews were against Paul. Why we've been taught that since we were children. But you see, Paul was never in our churches with their great literature, and he didn't know that the Jews were going to reject all that he was going to say. Do you think Paul was foolish enough to be preaching to people whom he knew would reject him? No, and that's why on one occasion Paul said to the Jews, in effect, "Let the blood be upon your hands, I'm going some place else to preach." But Paul went again to preach to the Jews. Paul was a Jew himself—and when he preached, he expected people to respond. You see, in some ways, it was a surprise to Paul that the Jews rejected him. You ask, Didn't Paul know that the Jews had rejected Jesus? Yes, but that was before the resurrection and to the apostle Paul the most important thing in the world was the resurrection because it was the resurrected Christ who appeared to him on the road to Damascus. He thought the Jews could be converted with the knowledge of the resurrection.

Paul thought the Jews would listen to him, and some of them did. Some of them responded. But his greatest opposition was not from Gallio of the civil court but from the religious people. You and I will find in our lives that, when we stand up for good and righteousness and Christ, trouble will come from some of the most unexpected sources. This is true in our nation today. Look at some of the unexpected sources that I feel trouble is coming from.

For one thing, trouble for you and for me is coming from a national attitude. I can remember the religious fervor of days gone by. I can remember so well men telling me of the great faith of the American people. There's a different national attitude than there was thirty-five years ago. Do you think for one moment that the approval of abortion and homosexuality could have come in the United States thirty-five years ago? Never! But today, the national attitude not only approves it but also encourages it.

Christians are not allowed to place the Ten Commandments in schools. In one school in the East, where the Ten Commandments were taken from the wall, on the same nail was placed a sign advertising a "love-in" that night after school.

In one state, at this very moment, there is a suit before the federal courts to outlaw the baccalaureate services in the schools. Our national attitude is not for Christ or the church. It's in opposition. And when you and I find ourselves in trouble with the national attitude, we are disturbed because we begin to wonder if we are the oddballs. When you find yourself in trouble with the national attitude that is in trouble with God, you stay in trouble with the national attitude.

Our nation goes where the people take it. If we begin joining the crowd of the crazy and the parade of the putrid, we're going to find our nation exactly like they want it. Now I don't want to live in a land of immoral people—living in filth. If you do, let your trouble bother you. But if you don't, live for Christ irrespective of the criticisms; live your life wholly, worthily, and irrespective of what's going to come because of it. You're going to be shocked when you find trouble in your life coming from the most unexpected sources.

The national attitude is not for Christ. It is against our Lord, and we must in some way overcome it. Institutions of higher learning are going to cause trouble for us if we stand up for

Christ. I am shocked by some of the institutions which bear the name Christian; some of them in the East that were started by people who loved Jesus Christ and made sacrifices for him are now strongholds of atheism and agnosticism and every doctrine in the world contrary to what Jesus Christ taught religiously, ethically, and morally.

Christianity is out-of-date some say. It's no use anymore. I hope that as long as God gives you and me strength to live and to preach and to teach that we'll live Christianity and preach, just like God wants us to.

The trouble with trouble is that is comes from unexpected sources. One of the most unexpected sources of trouble, when you live in Christ, is the church. Sometimes I'm shocked to pick up the newspaper and find out what the leader of some churches has said—what some preacher has said. You may find yourself crosswise with somebody's preaching, some doctrine—somebody who calls himself religious. Just overlook it, just go on, because that's the way trouble is. But that's the trouble with trouble. It comes from unexpected and sometimes surprising, disarming sources.

We May Deceive Ourselves About the Reality of Wrong

In verse 18, I find something that really holds my attention, "And Paul after this tarried there yet for awhile." I think I know what would have happened if I had been preaching to this congregation and they had done all of that to me. I might have prayed for a pulpit committee. But Paul didn't have that attitude; he "tarried there yet a good while."

Paul knew that when you get in trouble standing for what you believe, there is a tendency to deceive yourself about the value of your stand and you rationalize, "Well, maybe things aren't so bad. I still believe what I believe in. Everybody has a right to believe as they choose."

There is not a place in the Bible where Jesus said, "Mind

your own business." He said, to mind his business. And some of us, so concerned about keeping out of trouble with others, say, "Well, I think a person ought to mind his own business." You're not supposed to mind your own business as a Christian, you're supposed to be about the business of Jesus. And the business of Jesus Christ is telling others about him and being a witness. It's being an example. It's not being obnoxious. No. But it's living such a life and speaking such a word that when trouble comes from your stand, you won't say, "Things are about like they ought to be. It's wonderful. The world is just pleasant. Isn't it sweet how everybody is trying to do good."

This world is full of evil. This world is full of sin, and you and I must take our stand. We must be as willing as Paul was to stand and say, "It's not right, I know it's not, and I want to do something about it. The way of Christ is better."

A person interested in real Christianity will not be talked out of his convictions. He will be willing to pay the price of Christian excellence. Trouble will not derail him. He will, as his master, be willing to carry his cross to fulfill the will of God for his life.

21

The Best and the Blest

(Acts 18:24-28)

Look closely at Apollos. Notice the unfolding reality that sometimes the most blest people in the world are not giving their best. When a person approaches life, especially a person who is blest, he ought to approach life as a sacred trust.

Life is a gift. Life is something we did not ask for. It's something that we cannot initially refuse. Life is a gift of God. If you were to read the statistics of how many children are born into this world but do not live but a second, a minute, a few hours, a day, or a week, you would be astounded. Life is indeed a gift. This man, Apollos, about which we learn now, was a man that knew this; he was a man of ability, stature, education, and training. He was from the city of Alexandria. No one could live in Alexandria and compete unless he was a scholar. Alexandria was the stronghold of the Jews, and it was a place where men had a free liberal exchange of ideas. This man, Apollos, was one of the gigantic intellects of the most intellectually concentrated places in all of the New Testament era.

Apollos was a genius. He was an intellectual among intellectuals. He was a scholar's scholar and yet he appreciated the fact that life is a gift.

Please note the kind of man Apollos was. There just wasn't anybody in the Bible more capable, intellectually or academically, than Apollos. In fact, when you read some of the letters of Paul, you find that some people liked Apollos more than they liked Paul. Apollos could outspeak Paul. He was a man so tremendously endowed with the gifts and the talents of God that when he walked into a room crowded with people, every eye turned to him.

Notice something strange about him. He didn't get egotistical about his gifts and think that because he was gifted everyone else was nothing but dirt. This man of intellect and power knew that life was a sacred trust. He knew it was not a trust of the society, the state, not even a trust of mothers and fathers; life is a godly trust. People would say to Apollos, "Now Apollos, this is real silly—giving all of your time to the work of Jesus." Apollos must have thought to himself, as he looked at those people who questioned his dedication, and asked himself, Why was I born with a good body, broad shoulders, and a lot of gray matter between my ears. Why was I given all of this ability? For only one reason, he would answer himself, to bring glory and honor to my Lord, Jesus Christ.

Apollos was a man who could have used his ability to have been rich, to have been popular, to have been famous, to have had his name kept by his family as a man of great accomplishment, but he knew that life was a gift of God. Don't you wish every blest person were at his best like Apollos?

What if someone were to give you a million dollars and say, "Now this million dollars is yours and you may spend it to live. But I'm giving you a list of things that I want you to do with this million dollars. You'll have enough to live richly, but I just ask that you do particular things which are on this list." You fold the list and put it in your pocket and say, "Thank you for the million dollars." You never read the list. You ignored it.

What kind of gratitude would that be? You see, God has given us life. He's given us lungs. He's given us breath. He's given us hands and feet. He's given us eyes and ears. He says, "I give you a Book, you can live this life just like you want to live it. I'll make you rich in things that are important, but please obey my Book." Yet, like taking a million dollars and ignoring the request of the one who made you wealthy, you take God's gifts of life and salvation and ignore his Word—how pitifully ungrateful.

What are you doing with God's Book? Are you slapping the giver in the face and using the gift all for yourself? Apollos didn't. He was very blessed, very intellectual, very academic, and very dedicated. The first thing I'm saying is the blest person, especially, ought to realize that life is a sacred trust. Second of all,

Talent Cannot Replace Commitment

This is one of the most needed thoughts I can stress. Here was a man who was talented. He could speak and he could preach and the Scriptures say that he was "an eloquent man, and mighty in the scriptures" (v. 24). And then notice in verse 25, "and being fervent in the spirit, he spake and taught diligently." Here was a man who didn't think because he was talented he didn't have to be dedicated.

Let me illustrate what I'm trying to say. While in college, I had a couple of revivals with a young music man whom I suppose, was the finest solo voice in our university. As far as good looks is concerned, he was right at the top. He was suave, and his personality was second to none. And yet, when it came to being dedicated, he was not. He was a performer.

Christianity has no room for big shots. Christianity has no place for performers. It must have reformers. Yet, that's all my friend was. He was talented and so he thought that the man who works down at the plant and makes a few dollars a week could do all of the soul-winning. Let others be forgiving; let others not hold grudges; let others pray. And oh, how shocked I was to find in this man's heart a lack of dedication to Jesus Christ.

Talent is no excuse to get out of being dedicated to the Lord. Apollos didn't feel that way. I can imagine if he had gone to a brush arbor meeting, he would have gotten excited with everybody else. He would have said the loudest amen, for he was not only an eloquent man, but verse 25 tells the best thing about him—"being fervent in the spirit, he spake and taught diligently." Oh, it doesn't matter how well we can teach or how well we can preach or how well we can sing. If we're not dedicated, we are as sounding brass or tinkling cymbal. We have nothing at all unless we are dedicated to the total truth of God's Word.

Once a man came to the First Baptist Church of Dallas and was looking for Dr. Truett, and the secretary said, "Why, Dr. Truett has gone to see one of our shut-ins, Mrs. Rayburn."

The man said, "Why, I just must see Dr. Truett—it's so important."

The secretary said, "I can tell you where Mrs. Rayburn lives." She gave him the needed directions.

This man got into his car and followed the directions the secretary had given him. He knocked on Mrs. Rayburn's door and nobody came to the door. Finally, he noticed someone around back, and he went around to the back of the house and the little old lady was standing there. He saw a coat hanging on the outside on the door knob. He inquired, "Mrs. Rayburn, I'm so and so and I'm looking for Dr. Truett. I hear he was visiting you."

She said, "Yes, he is, he's out back." So he went out back and there Dr. Truett with white hair, tall stature, the epitome of dignity, a man more talented, probably, than any other preacher in the Southern Baptist Convention, who had taken off his coat and was out sawing wood in the midst of the cold winter for this woman. He would carry the wood into her house to burn for fuel.

We don't need more eloquent preachers, we don't need more polished sopranos, we just don't need more capable teachers. We need people with love that pulsates in their hearts. We need people with a spirit that can win the world. We need people who are fervent and diligent and use their blest abilities for God with all of their hearts and souls. I found, long ago, that people will overlook a flop in a sermon more than they will a failure of care and concern and love. It will be so for you. Talent can never replace commitment and dedication to Jesus. Apollos knew that. That's why he was fervent. That's why he was diligent.

A Willingness to Improve

Apollos, with all of his eloquence and all of his intellectual power and all of his ability to speak, was a man who didn't know what he ought to know. He was baptized by John the Baptist, and as far as Apollos knew, that was all that was necessary. For Apollos from Alexandria (Alexandria's Jewish school) believed in interpreting Scripture apocolyptically, which meant that when the Jews of Alexandria read the Old Testament they not only looked for the meaning historically, they looked for a further meaning—a secondary meaning—an apocalyptical meaning. They knew that there was something else besides a historical account of the nation of Israel.

Apollos believed that, so he had come to the conclusion that Jesus was indeed the Messiah of which the Old Testament Scripture taught so fervently, but he didn't know Jesus as Savior. He knew what it was to know Jesus historically, but he didn't know how to have Jesus as a living presence and power in his life.

Aquilla and Priscilla took Apollos home with them. They began to tell him, "Now, we're going to tell you about God more perfectly." Apollos could have said, "Now wait a moment, you people haven't got the degrees that I have. You're not as trained as I am. You're not as dedicated as I am. Who are you to tell me what I must do?" But he listened and he learned.

Sometimes people with ability are sensitive to being told that they just might could be better. That attitude is not best. Do you have that attitude? I knew a lady in one of the churches I pastored who had such a difficult problem in her life that we asked a committee to go see her and help. Her problem was ripping out the roots of our church. We didn't want that because our church was having a good fellowship. A group of men went and said they wanted to pray with her and help her. They were as kind as anyone could have been.

The lady reacted violently. She went on a rampage. A lady we had known as talented and kind, used words of profanity to express her anger. She just could not imagine that she could be improved at all.

The blest people of this world need to be the best. "For unto whomsoever much is given, of him shall be much required," says the Bible (Luke 12:48). That not only means that the particular talent is to be used but also the total life is to be wholly submitted to the lordship of Jesus Christ!

About the Author

Dr. Bailey E. Smith is pastor of First Southern Baptist Church, Del City, Oklahoma, the second largest church in the Southern Baptist Convention. Since Smith became pastor, the church has grown from 6,600 members to over 12,000. The church has led the SBC in baptisms for several years, and Smith baptized over 1,000 persons per year three of his first five years there.

Two of his earlier pastorates were First Church, Warren, Arkansas, and First Church, Hobbs, New Mexico. He has served as president of the SBC Pastors Conference and on the nominating committee of the SBC. He has written for several periodicals and has authored three books.

He was educated at Ouachita Baptist University and Southwestern Baptist Theological Seminary. He has honorary degrees from Ouachita and Southwest Baptist College.

He and his wife, Sandra, have three sons, Scott, Steven, and Josh.

HAVE YOU READ . . .
REAL EVANGELISM ? ? ?
EVANGELIST BILLY GRAHAM says: "Everybody should read this book!"

This book by Bailey E. Smith is like a two-edged sword—because of its thrust based on the written Word of God. It cuts, burns, and stings, but it is penned from a heart of compassion and *agapé* love.

He writes: "My prayer is that *Real Evangelism* will awaken all who read it to a new joy of sharing their faith. If this happens, the purpose of this book will have been fulfilled."

Smith is alarmed that many Christian activities and programs—while good in themselves—are taking the place of genuine, New Testament evangelism.

"Yet they are becoming substitutes, and the trend is extremely dangerous and very damaging to the fulfillment of the Great Commission. The devil provides substitutes in subtle ways, and we gladly receive them, hoping to relieve our guilt for not being involved in leading others to know Jesus. Millions have fallen victim to that process!"

Real Evangelism is definitely an exposé book that should stir evangelical Christians.